THE

UNLIMITED POWER WITHIN YOU

KARIN HADADAN

THOUGHT CATALOG Books

THOUGHTCATALOG.COM

**THOUGHT
CATALOG
Books**

Published by Thought Catalog Books, an imprint of Thought Catalog, a digital magazine owned and operated by The Thought & Expression Co. Inc., an independent media organization founded in 2010 and based in the United States of America. For stocking inquiries, contact stockists@shopcatalog.com.

Produced by Chris Lavergne and Noelle Beams
Art direction and design by KJ Parish
Creative editorial direction by Brianna Wiest
Circulation management by Isidoros Karamitopoulos

thoughtcatalog.com | shopcatalog.com

International edition, printed internationally and fulfilled by Amazon in select countries. The limited, original print edition remains available to order and ships worldwide from ShopCatalog.com.

ISBN 978-1-949759-88-4

For those who have yet to believe in themselves,
may these words be the catalyst.

INTRODUCTION

In 'The Architecture of Happiness,' Alain de Botton pens a line that resonates with the soul: *"It is perhaps when our lives are at their most problematic that we are likely to be most receptive to beautiful things."* This phrase found me at 19 years old, a beacon in my desire for depth and meaning, as I sought to fulfill an inner thirst for understanding on what true happiness means. Little could I have anticipated that it would be amid a series of health challenges and a descent to life's nadir that the truth of his words would crystalize for me. It was in the midst of adversity that I truly comprehended the power of beauty to heal, to inspire, and to transform. That realization became a pivotal moment of awakening—where the most intricate depths of life's design are revealed not only in ease, but also in the complex, often painful moments of our personal journeys.

I believe that our quest into the realms of creativity, spirituality, and personal growth is born from an essential need. It is not until we face pivotal moments of challenge that we are compelled to seek inner and Divine truth. The traditional approaches of Western culture cease to serve us and shallow remedies lose their allure—we are called to unearth the depths of our being, to uproot the hidden maladies that tarnish our spirit, and illuminate the unseen light that can revitalize our souls. Answering this call is just the beginning; true fulfillment blossoms not from solitary insights but from transforming our tribulations into a higher calling. It is in sharing our hard-earned wisdom for the betterment of all that we discover the purest form of inner peace and fulfillment.

The genesis of this book materialized in the turbulent period following my surgery to remove Endometriosis—a disease that eluded detection throughout my life, yet stood as the silent architect of my numerous health struggles for over a decade. This illness, I came to realize, was not just a physical ailment but a manifestation of a lifetime spent in a relentless state of fight or flight and emotional dis-ease, a bitter realization that I had unintentionally nurtured the seeds of my own suffering, despite living a very mindful life.

In the wake of surgery, I grappled with feelings of defeat, pondered the efficacy of the procedure, and wrestled with doubts about the destiny God had laid out for me. Having surmounted myriad debilitating health battles since the age of twelve, I had anticipated this surgery to be the definitive and immediate turning point. I experienced many Divine signs from my spirits above that this surgery was the answer to all of my prayers. They were right in the end, however, fate carved out a more turbulent path for me to get there, a voyage where each day called for a deep spiritual awakening, challenging and expanding the horizons of my being. It became clear that my path to wellness—both physical and emotional—would stretch further than my patience had room for. But amidst this uncontrollable journey, a deep-seated intuition whispered to me that the revelations emerging from my ordeal would ignite the spark for this book—one destined to bring about profound healing, for myself, and for countless others. Thus, I leaned into it.

Echoing the wisdom of Alain de Botton, it was through my darkest trials that my heart opened up, inviting an outpouring of blessings that defied logical comprehension. I felt an unprecedented closeness to the Divine, not merely as a warmth within my chest but as a tangible presence in the chance encounters and life-altering conversations with strangers, in the magical orchestration of new connections, in serendipitous experiences that revealed themselves as guiding lights, in song lyrics that struck a chord, and in the inspiring works of other authors. The beauty that I opened myself up to began to overpower the shadows that I faced.

The following pages are a collection of the raw thoughts, surges of emotion, visceral feelings, and Divine insights that accompanied me on my path to healing. These words are not post-realizations; they are real-time reflections captured as I navigated the intense waters of each day, a chronicle of my evolution, cementing each step of growth as it unfolded. This narrative served as my vessel to honor the wisdom I was absorbing, guiding me to not only become the woman I envisioned but also to embrace the innocence of the girl I once was.

Embedded in every passage I write is a silent mantra, a promise from the Universe: *"You may not understand now, but someday you will."* The road to such understanding was long and woven with countless meditations, intentional breaths, shed tears, joyful laughs, acts of surrendering and heartfelt prayers. Each step on this journey was a lesson in patience and trust, a testament to the strength that resides within us even when it lies dormant. My journey was a crucible, transforming uncertainty into wisdom, pain into resilience, and experience into enlightenment.

If this book has reached your hands, it is a clear sign that God has chosen you for an awakening, a deliberate summons to rise into your full potential. My wish for this creation is for it to be more than mere words on a page; it is a shared experience, a communion of souls. I aim to touch the very essence of your being, to resonate with the silent struggles and the unspoken dreams that live within you. This is not just a book; it is a vessel for transformation, a call to awaken the powerful and Holy force that resides in each of you. Let these pages be a mirror reflecting your own potential, a beacon illuminating the path to your higher self. May my words serve as a catalyst, empowering you to release the boundless strength within and to rise, with grace and sovereignty, to the magnificence of your destined place in the world.

Thank you for being here. I hope you enjoy it.

With love and gratitude,
Karin Hadadan

PART 1

AWAKENING THE SELF

The Chosen Ones

Spiritual awakenings are often experienced out of necessity; our souls sense that our potential transcends the limitations of our current challenges. We feel called to go deeper—inwards and within—towards a path that was predestined, waiting for us to explore it in Divine timing.

As we enter this new world, we will see that what was once only known as our suffering will soon become the initiation into our higher selves and the portal towards our higher purpose. To have the opportunity to reawaken our authentic being, let go of our limited beliefs, rediscover what we've forgotten, reconnect with who we always were, heal ourselves and heal others, is the gift of our lifetimes.

Although it may be daunting here and there, where your strength and resilience may be tested, you must continue to embrace it. Because your new life awaits, on the other side.

Beauty in the Stillness

The paradox is that the biggest epiphanies bloom in the sacred garden of stillness. When you choose to step away from the outer world and instead tap into the silence that lies within, you begin to wander towards a journey of deep understanding that decodes the chaos around you.

In this transformative odyssey, you come to a powerful realization: what appeared as external disruption was, in fact, a mirror reflecting the turbulence within. The chaos was never an external force; it was a dynamic echo of your own internal landscape, a revelation that can empower you to navigate and transcend the tumult with newfound courage and grit.

This understanding forms the belief that the answers you seek already lie within you.

Wounds can only heal with the truth.

Every new day is an invitation to reveal something about yourself that you have unknowingly been disassociating from. Within the recesses of your soul, if you detect an emptiness, an aching wound, a haze over your thoughts, a lack of direction, or a bitterness tainting your heart—these are poignant reminders that your current existence diverges from the vibrational rhythm your soul yearns to embrace.

Repeatedly, life will cast you into the same intricate patterns until you understand the underlying reasons sustaining them. You'll attract similar individuals until you recognize the driving force behind their gravitational pull. Undesirable outcomes will persist until you uncover the subconscious beliefs tied to your goals. Our habitual cycles, relationships, and consequences often mirror facets of ourselves we've suppressed for too long. These concealed aspects may echo our hunger for control, a thirst for admiration or attention, or stem from a lack of self-worth, self-love, and self-awareness.

Yet, the challenge lies in the fact that these concealed elements don't confine themselves to isolated corners of our lives—they permeate every endeavor and every individual we encounter. The control over our relationships spreads towards regulating our eating habits or by restricting our emotions. The quest for attention may initiate through a toxic relationship but ripples into how we present ourselves online or engage in social gatherings. The deficit in self-worth may cast its shadow over a stagnant career but it then extends into friendships lacking boundaries or a partnership falling short of meeting our genuine needs. The hidden part, the one we've evaded, stands as the wellspring of almost every unfavorable outcome in our lives.

Once you unravel the why behind your actions, a new path unfolds before you. Envision it as the commencement of a trail, each step leading to a destination that initially appears elusive but is, in truth, a journey filled with breathtaking views and enlightening experiences. As you take your first step, shedding light on what you've concealed, you'll find yourself compelled to continue walking forward. The allure of discovering more, the anticipation of where it leads, and the revelation of the root source of your suffering beckon you to delve deeper into the labyrinth of self-discovery.

As time unfolds, clarity surfaces across the meaning behind all of your actions. You unravel the threads that led you to a certain path—a path filled with the echoes of an unhealed childhood wound, the lingering shadows of projections from those you held dear, or the whispers of a long-buried traumatic experience. But in a revelation as luminous as daylight, you realize that the shackles of your past don't have to dictate your future. It is within this transformative moment that the truth emerges as both the soothing balm for your innermost wounds and the liberating force that unfurls the wings of your spirit.

The truth becomes not just the healer but the liberator of your soul.

REALIZE THAT EVERY
NUANCE OF SUFFERING
AND JOY HAS BEEN A
DELIBERATE STROKE IN
THE MASTERPIECE OF
YOUR LIFE, AN ESSENTIAL
PRELUDE TO THE AWE-
INSPIRING CHAPTER
YET TO BE WRITTEN.

John 13:7

In this significant season of your life, it's as though God is meticulously crafting you for the extraordinary journey that awaits. Each door ready to swing open, every upcoming experience, and each prayer on the brink of fulfillment are the essential threads stitching together the story of your life. What comes next would not make sense had you not navigated the depths of your recent trials. Realize that every nuance of suffering and joy has been a deliberate stroke in the masterpiece of your life, an essential prelude to the awe-inspiring chapter yet to be written.

At times, the echoing questions of *"What is the purpose of this?"* and *"What are you trying to teach me?"* will reverberate in your mind. Amidst these moments, even in Divine silence, God remains unwaveringly faithful to His promises. He is not indifferent or unresponsive; rather, He is your guiding force, a shield and mentor, sculpting your faith and trust. These experiences are purposefully granted to vitalize your patience and fuel the dormant strength within you.

If every wish of yours was granted instantaneously, the person you're becoming would lack the depth and resilience shaped by the passage of time. This version of yourself, born from the amalgamation of suffering and joy, is a testament to your extraordinary metamorphosis. Cherish this empowered self, for it embodies the triumphs of your journey, a resilient spirit, and a strength you might never have known existed—an incarnation of yourself, undoubtedly, not to be traded for anything in the world.

"Oh my God," I say, as I take it all in.

There is a reason why we all verbalize this phrase so often, and it is quite simple—we can find divinity everywhere.

In the gentle caress of sunlight upon a serene river, witness God's reminder that tranquility reflects the brilliance of Divine light. As we gaze across distant mountains, we feel the heartbeat of a journey yet to be conquered, a testament to the heights He knows we can reach. In the laughter of someone cherished, embrace the melody of love orchestrated by God Himself.

Savoring the juiciness of fresh fruit on a warm summer morning, we taste the sweetness woven into the fabric of simplicity. Nestling our heads upon a loved one's shoulder, we discover God's affirmation that within this vast world, there exists a sanctuary of safety and solace.

He dwells in all of humanity, in the deep conversations that grace our paths, in the harmonies of the songs that resonate with our souls, in the written words that stir our spirits, within our own souls. His presence threads through the landscapes we explore, the cinematic tales that unfold before us, and the very garments that clothe us.

Recognizing that He surrounds you and resides within, how could you ever doubt being guided by a cosmic force? He communicates through subtle whispers, painting the world with His inherent essence. Open your eyes to the Divine fingerprints on everything you touch, for in each encounter lies a message from the Creator, a revelation of His Divine touch upon your existence.

He is here, there, everywhere. And perhaps, so are you.

Act One

Inhale. Exhale. Be where your feet are. Look around you. Experience this very moment in its entirety. Embrace the life you have been given. Observe the life you've created for yourself. Take note of the people in your sphere, the success you've facilitated, the body you've strengthened, the mind you've nurtured, and the heart you've expanded. Be aware of the words you speak, the thoughts you think, and the actions you partake in.

You are a unique soul living in a human body and you have been given the rare opportunity to design a vibrant life, one filled with pure joy, peace, and euphoria, one where you can do anything and be anyone. Remember, you are the architect of your destiny, the author of your story. Embrace the power that pulses within your veins, the courage that resides in your heart. For you are not a mere spectator in the theater of existence, you are the star on the stage of your own life's play.

Inhale. Exhale. You are alive. You are here.

Now, go forth and conquer.

GREATER GRATITUDE
FOR WHAT WE ALREADY
POSSESS BRINGS GREATER
PEACE FOR WHAT IS
YET TO BE REALIZED.

Greater gratitude for what we already possess
brings greater peace for what is yet to be realized.

Sometimes, the anticipation for your prayers to be answered makes the minutes feel like hours, the hours feel like weeks, and the weeks feel like years. But in those in-between periods, where impatience takes over and frustration begins, you must not forget to notice the blessings God has already given you. The love you give and receive, moments you couldn't stop laughing, friends checking in, new connections that foster fulfillment, a blossomed career, healing that's taken place, travels across the world and time given to rest. You must not forget to recognize how these were once among the things you used to pray for.

**There is intentionality hidden in
the simple ways we exist.**

Every second, your eyes gracefully open and close. This rhythmic dance is not merely a spectacle; it's the essence of clarity. Without these effortless blinks, the canvas of your sight would lack the vital strokes that keep it vibrant and focused.

In order to breathe, your chest undergoes a series of movements to facilitate the intake of air into your lungs—the muscles create changes in pressure within the chest cavity, in order to inhale and exhale air that allows you to continue existing.

In constant motion, your hands effortlessly weave between opening and closing. This perpetual dance is more than mere movement; it is the very antidote to paralysis. Without this symphony of gestures, the vibrant expression and functionality of your hands would be stilled.

There is a balance and coordination embedded in your daily functions, revealing the beauty inherent in each small contraction and expansion. As human beings, we cannot continue to exist or live without these fluctuations, therefore what purpose is there to resist the changes that arrive in our daily lives? Is the way in which we were created not proof enough that the contractions and expansions we face are all deliberate?

Some Kinda Heaven

When life feels like a catastrophic symphony—where pain suffuses your entire body, confusion fills your mind, and anger lingers in your heart, allow yourself to sit back, do nothing, and observe. These are the instances where life is trying to teach you something.

When life feels like a blissful harmony—where euphoria permeates through your entire soul, serenity penetrates your mind and peace spreads within your heart, allow yourself to sit back, do nothing, and absorb. These are the instances where life is trying to offer you something.

The diverse states in which you experience your life are equally filled with beautiful truths. The contrasting circumstances provide various degrees of blessings, but each one is there for an intentional purpose. Some experiences urge you to look within, others compel you to look above. Some moments force you to confront your deepest fears, others invite you to embrace your greatest joys. Some events propel you to surrender your control, others inspire you to take action.

This truthful understanding teaches you to embody ever-lasting peace, by believing that you are always where you're supposed to be. If you were meant to be somewhere else or experiencing something else, you'd be there already. With a heart that is open to receiving—whether it be a challenging lesson or a pleasant gift—a state of tranquility washes over you, accepting that the current step of your journey is unfolding exactly as it should.

Ebbs & Flows

Throughout each hardship, you will be given subtle opportunities to laugh again, feel joy again, and feel love again. Although it might seem fleeting at the moment, this is the Universe's way of saying: "*It will be okay again. You will feel like yourself again. You will rise again. Again, and again, and again.*"

Divine Timing

If you woke up tomorrow morning and all that you were left with were things you thanked God for yesterday, what would you have?

If you woke up tomorrow morning and you were handed every single thing you prayed to God for yesterday, would you even be able to hold all of it?

Navigate the stream of your days with gratitude as your strength and patience as your guide. For in this state of grace, your faith becomes unshakable, where you trust that everything you are seeking will be provided at the exact moment you are not only ready to receive it, but also hold and carry it forward.

The Universe is always conspiring in your favor.

Each time I stood at life's crossroads, perplexed on which path to take, it was through an open prayer that the most Divine guidance was revealed to me. I ceased to request for specific outcomes, recognizing that my own definitions of what I needed often limited the breadth of what I could receive. My mornings started off with a quiet whisper, *"Show me where to go, what to do, who to speak to, what to say, and what to hear."* This prayer became a beacon of hope—illuminating the trust I placed in the day's journey, confident that the tools for my evolution would be handed to me seamlessly.

The openness to the Universe's will led me to act in miraculous ways—researching subjects I had no prior knowledge in that offered new insights on suppressed emotions, stumbling upon old songs with lyrics that mirrored the exact guidance I yearned for, advocating for myself when my doctors assured me that everything looked normal, seeking wisdom from experts in fields I was now exploring, embracing novel modalities for healing, moving my body even when I had no energy in efforts to revitalize myself, being spontaneously placed in new environments that provoked inspiration, and engaging with strangers who were vessels for messages the Divine was trying to communicate with me.

As I let go of the reins towards my healing, ceasing to control the outcome, the Universe revealed uncharted paths for me to explore. But the Universe didn't just respond—it conspired in my favor, healing me in ways I couldn't have envisioned, soothing the unknown aches of my soul. It taught me that when we surrender our need to steer the healing, we allow the vastness of the cosmos to guide us to wholeness, to heal not just what we know is broken but also what we are oblivious to.

And that is the greatest thing that can happen to us.

THE WISEST THING WE CAN LEARN IS TO KNOW ENOUGH TO KNOW THAT WE DON'T ACTUALLY KNOW EVERYTHING.

Surrendering is not a mere absence of fear; it's a raw, heart-wrenching embrace of uncertainty, a courageous stance that clings to the enduring belief of the benevolent flow of life. It's the unwavering faith that, despite the onslaught of obstacles, you still trust that everything is unfolding in a way uniquely tailored for you. It's the resilience to keep maintaining hope, even when the harsh reality offers no tangible proof that you're treading the right path, through persistence in prayer amidst emotional and physical exhaustion. It's a constant interrogation of doubt, challenging shadows with the resounding question, *"What proof do I have that this is true?"* It's the soul-stirring act of expressing gratitude in the face of relentless challenges, when life seems to offer no respite or coherent meaning.

Because true surrender is a declaration you choose to make hundreds of times a day: *"Even if my eyes can't discern the way, I choose to still believe that something better awaits. I release the grip on my perceived needs and desires, allowing the Universe to usher in what is meant for me, unveiling its Divine plan at its own perfect time."*

Blank Canvas

Our limited awareness of the future isn't a flaw; it's a deliberate design. The intricacies of life unfold in a way that eludes our complete understanding, and there's a deeper purpose to this uncertainty. Imagine a world where the script of our lives was laid bare before us—every challenge, every twist, and every triumph revealed in advance. It would be a narrative devoid of intrigue, a tale lacking suspense and surprise. It would likely instill unnecessary fear, anxiety, and stress in the present moment, preventing us from taking action.

The beauty lies in the enigma of the unknown, the unrevealed chapters that make our journey captivating. How dull would life be if we held the blueprint of our destiny in our hands? The anticipation, the uncertainty, the struggle—these are elements that together craft a story of depth and significance. Our experiences gain value precisely because we navigate through the labyrinth of the unknown, adapting as needed.

Embrace the mystery, for it is the canvas on which we paint a life that is not just lived but passionately created. In this unpredictable dance of existence, every unexpected turn adds vibrancy, every challenge bestows wisdom, and every moment contributes to the masterpiece we are sculpting. Our lives become a collection of the unforeseen, and it is in this unpredictability that we find the raw, unfiltered beauty of our lives.

EMBRACE THE MYSTERY,
FOR IT IS THE CANVAS
ON WHICH WE PAINT
A LIFE THAT IS NOT
JUST LIVED BUT
PASSIONATELY CREATED.

Source

In the moments when the loud repetition of thoughts echoes through your mind, ask yourself a simple question: *"Whose voice is this?"* Feel the weight of that inquiry, for within it lies the power to unravel the threads of your inner dialogue. It's an exploration into the depths of your soul, a journey to unveil the origin of the whispers that shape your consciousness.

In that crucial instant, you'll witness a revelation unfolding—a sudden clarity like the first light breaking through a stormy sky. The words that weave through your thoughts may bear the imprints of your intuition, the chatter of your ego, the Divine echoes of God, the input of your parents' wisdom, the opinions of your friends' counsel, the tender murmurs of your beloved, the expressions of your colleagues' perspectives, or the pervasive influence of your social feed. Every utterance finds its origin, each voice a distinct thread in your psyche.

As you stand at the crossroads of self-discovery, there lies a choice—profound and transformative. With newfound awareness, you hold the key to detachment. Acknowledge the source, for in doing so, you gain the strength to disentangle yourself from any external or egoic voices that may cloud the authenticity of your soul's voice, and instead, get clarity on what your intuition or the Divine is expressing. It is a liberating act, a reclaiming of the reins of your own narrative. For in the hush that follows, you emerge not only as the curator of your thoughts but also as the architect of your own truth.

Recalibration

At the end of the day, ultimately you are the only one who knows what is right for you. Gather insights from those around you, seek their wisdom on which roads to take, when to voice your truth or embrace silence, when to leap forward or step away, but also understand that their counsel reflects their journey, not yours. They've had a different life's path, filled with various degrees of lessons and experiences, and so their perspectives, though well-intentioned, are through the lens of their own saga—a saga you have not lived. They cannot fully grasp the whispers of your heart, the ponderings of your mind, or the yearnings of your soul. Words, no matter how eloquently you string them together, cannot encapsulate the extent of your spirit's blueprint. Seek guidance, yes, but never forget: the most reliable compass is your inner voice. It might stray momentarily, but its true north remains constant, always ready to recalibrate you back to your destined path.

The Home Inside

First, we think. Then, we feel a feeling that reinforces that thought. Then, we act in a certain way that brings that feeling to life. It's the repetition of these thoughts that molds the clay of belief, shaping the very core of who we become, a powerful force for both better and worse. To redefine your reality, to sculpt the experiences and encounters that fill your days, you must start with questioning the thoughts that echo within to then rewrite the script of your subconscious beliefs.

Instead of pleading, *"Why is this happening to me?"* courageously ask, *"What lesson is this teaching me?"* Reject the crippling chant of *"I'm not enough"* and boldly affirm, *"I have always been sufficient and complete."* Drown out the whispers of *"I'm not lovable"* with the resounding truth, *"I am deserving of love and embrace myself fully."* Instead of succumbing to the despairing echo, *"I'll never heal from this,"* redirect your focus by declaring, *"My heart and body are resilient, constantly mending imbalances."* Refuse the defeatist narrative of *"Nothing is working out,"* and boldly assert, *"Things are unfolding in my favor, a silent dance behind the scenes."*

Take a moment to pause and contemplate: if you were to think in this altered state, how different would you feel? What actions would you partake in and what would you stop doing? How would you carry yourself? What boundaries would you place? Who would you walk away from, and who would you create space for?

In this turbulent symphony of thoughts, remember: you hold the power to choose which ones resonate and which ones you nurture. Your agency is a beacon, guiding you to shift perspectives and attitudes, offering the alchemy to transform how you perceive and engage with the circumstances of your life.

Meditating with your eyes open.

For years now, every single day, I've immersed myself in the sacred act of meditation. It's become more than just a practice; it's woven into the very fabric of my existence, infusing my life with a depth of joy I never knew possible. Each morning, I not only find solace in this ritual but also wake up craving it. It's a sanctuary where I retreat to reflect, to realign, and to recenter myself amidst the chaos of life.

In the gentle embrace of meditation, I grant myself the gift of introspection. It's a journey inward, where I reconnect with the essence of who I am and envision the person I strive to become. In this sacred space, I release the burdens of the past and let go of all that no longer serves me. Here, I am free to embrace stillness, to listen intently for the whispers of the Divine, and to commune with my inner wisdom.

When I share with others the early hours I dedicate to meditation, I'm often met with disbelief. *"How do you have the time?"* they ask, unable to comprehend the commitment. Yet, these same individuals marvel at the harmony I've cultivated in my life, even whilst navigating a journey of healing. They wonder at the seemingly effortless balance I strike between career, creativity, and self-care, and how I have transformed my state of being to one filled with lightness, faith, and love. They haven't connected the dots that it is through meditation that I have created the vibrant and aligned life I now live.

The truth is, there are no shortcuts on the path to inner peace. It's a journey that demands dedication and unwavering commitment—an investment I make in myself each and every day. So, when questioned about my resolve, I offer a simple truth: once you taste the transformative power of stillness, time becomes a triviality. Everything else becomes secondary and pales in comparison to the profound shifts it catalyzes within.

There is a misconception, however, that meditation is merely a fleeting escape into tranquility. The reality, however, is that it's not an escape but a doorway to conscious living. It's about being awakened—not only to the quietude of our minds, but also to the existence that surrounds us. Because once you are fully awake, the moment you step off of the cushion or the bed, you become a Divine creator and are able to notice the number of extraordinary things that exist around and within you.

So, as I start each new day, I do so with eyes, ears, and my heart wide open with the radiance of possibility. For in the sacred practice of meditation, I've discovered the true essence of being alive—a boundless journey of awakening to the miracles that await in every moment.

THE ONLY WAY TO
EXPERIENCE FREEDOM IS
TO BE AWARE OF WHAT
PART OF YOURSELF
YOU'RE TRYING TO
BE FREED FROM.

Know Thyself

How do you really turn your life around? It starts with truly knowing yourself. It's about being in tune with who you are, understanding your choices, your patterns, your beliefs, your personality, your emotions, your triggers, your dreams, and your reasons for doing things. It's not just about looking in the mirror; it's about looking deep inside yourself. It's asking those tough questions and challenging the answers you thought you knew. It's about wondering how you ended up where you are and questioning the beliefs that shaped your current reality. It's about noticing what provokes you and dissecting what unhealed wound is connected to it. It's about spending time thinking about what truly fulfills you and analyzing what part of you is holding you back from acting in accordance. It's about being aware of your addictions and looking into what suppressed emotions they're feeding.

The only way to experience freedom is to be aware of what part of yourself you're trying to be freed from. So you must decide—will you dive into the depths of your own existence and get clarity or would you prefer to stay in the comfort of where you are and continue living your life as it is?

When you choose to break free from the chains of your past and embrace a vision of your future, the unknown transforms from a source of fear into an exhilarating quest. You begin to feel excitement towards the moments of revelation, the enchanting magic, the soul-soothing exhales, the radiant enlightenment, and the thrilling discoveries that lie ahead.

Once you get a taste of freedom, I promise, you won't ever look back, because the allure of what lies ahead becomes an irresistible force constantly propelling you forward.

The only way out is through.

There are some paths that lead us to a dead end. We find ourselves trapped in circles, yearning for a hidden passage that might guide us to a brighter destination. Instead of focusing on the visible exit, we choose to tread wearily along the same path, passing by familiar faces, reliving the same moments, and seeing unchanged views. Often, we don't even realize we're wandering aimlessly in circles, as it has become our familiar, although exhausting, rhythm.

Perhaps the only escape is retracing our steps to the beginning. Exiting through the entrance we once entered, we return to the origin—by delving into introspection, confronting past traumas, and deepening our understanding of ourselves.

What if in walking backward toward the start, we uncover what was once overlooked or unnoticed and rediscover what we've long forgotten? What if *this* is the new path we've been searching for?

It's been there all along—simply waiting for us to step into it.

The Glitch Phase

Entering the space where your life falls short of the boundless potential pulsating within you is an emotionally charged journey. It's like navigating a realm where the reality you inhabit doesn't fully align with the magnitude of your inner essence. An unsettling discomfort and painful sensation permeates your entire being, as though you're experiencing a glitch in your own life.

You might notice that some parts of your life are shaping up just as you imagined—they're aligning with your vision. On the flip side, there are areas where you haven't quite reached that point yet. You're on the right path, making the right moves, and taking actions that align with your goals. Still, it feels like you're consistently approaching the destination without ever quite reaching it.

Only those who have dreams can fathom this disconnect. It's not that your life is devoid of joy or success, nor that you lack elements of your aspirations, nor that you believe you aren't deserving of a better life. It's an indescribable yearning, an ache for the moment where your current reality matches the entire truth that pulses within you.

In the metaphorical video game of life, perhaps there's a silver lining to these glitches—they serve as challenges that, when navigated, cultivate reflection. They grant us access to areas of our life that would typically remain unexplored, prompting us to adapt and thrive in the face of unexpected twists. If we're never compelled to pause and appreciate our achievements, how can we cultivate gratitude when we enter the next level? Without these glitches prompting us to acknowledge our present, we might find ourselves in some distant future plagued by guilt for not being thankful for the levels we've already achieved.

These intentional interruptions not only guide us to explore the hidden or unfinished content of our present-day existence but also shape us into more resilient beings, capable of overcoming the challenges that arise in our near future.

The Gift of Time

They say that time heals all wounds, but society falls short in explaining why that holds true within every chapter of life—in moments of loss, health struggles, or heartbreak.

What they often omit is this simple truth—it's only when we grant ourselves the grace of time that we unravel wisdom, find enlightenment, and stumble upon revelations that eventually mend the fractures within. With each passing moment, we're presented with the chance to glean insights from our past. It might be a sudden realization, a moment of clarity, or a quiet understanding that whispers, *"Ah, that's why things unfolded that way,"* or, *"That's the lesson I needed to learn."* It's the gradual discovery of layers within ourselves, mending the silent pains of our souls.

These transformative moments don't manifest overnight; how could they? How could we connect the dots of weeks, months, or years in the blink of an eye? How could we fully embrace the emotions needed for a massive rebirth in just 24 hours? Our bodies wield immense power, yet, to gather new wisdom, we must shed the weight of old thoughts and beliefs. So, is it fair to demand of ourselves to undergo this intricate process of learning and unlearning within the confines of a fleeting moment?

Instead, these revelations manifest as we evolve, grow, and navigate the ebb and flow of life. Time heals all wounds because, in the matrix of time, we encounter the threads of understanding that weave together our healing journey. It's a gradual unfolding, an ongoing dance with life's rhythms that gradually stitches the torn pieces of our hearts. Time is the gentle sculptor, molding us into stronger, wiser versions of ourselves, and in this patient evolution, we experience the true magic of healing.

Rock Bottom

There I was, on my knees, imploring the heavens to take everything I cherished. I pleaded with God to take away my home, my wardrobe, my jewels, my riches, my triumphs, my career, my community, if only He would grant me the gift of radiant health. I was prepared to surrender it all, negotiating and sacrificing every tangible treasure at the altar of normalcy and well-being.

The true impact of trauma remains elusive until it becomes a haunting part of your own story. In that poignant realization, everything else fades away and the stark truth emerges: nothing else in this world truly mattered. No possession, no accolade, no accomplishment could ever measure up to the irreplaceable value of one's health.

As I begged, *"God, I allow you to take it all away. Please, just take everything I have away and grant me radiant health,"* I heard a tender murmur from a voice that was not mine. That was the moment I noticed God's echo, where He whispered, *"I don't need to strip you of these treasures, for I gave them to you. And now, in your quest for restoration, I promise you, I will provide abundantly. In every facet of your existence, I will provide you with the richness of true well-being."*

Which shattered piece of my soul convinced me that I couldn't have it all? With tears streaming down my face, I welcomed the promise of abundance with an unwavering trust. The Creator, who witnessed my silent struggles and was aware of the destination I aspired to reach, became my anchor. My story, once marked by anguish, would unfold as a testament to the miracles born of unyielding faith, both in Him and myself, revealing a new level of spiritual awakening and new way of living.

Quantum Leap

What if I told you that the reason why you want certain things so deeply is because it's already yours at some point on the timeline? Your future self is whispering to you through intuitive feelings, dreams planted deep within, and crystal-clear visions. Those desires are not just wants; they're previews of what's already yours on the timeline of your life. Embody them in this present moment, for they are the breadcrumbs leading you to the manifestation of your destiny.

Rome wasn't built in a day.

Your patience will continuously be tested with what your heart desires the most. If your heart yearns for financial success, you will find yourself entangled in experiences where economic freedom seems elusive, all aimed at forging a character capable of achieving and sustaining prosperity. Dreaming of a fulfilling marriage? You'll encounter individuals who may not meet your exact standards, guiding you towards understanding not only what you want but also what you truly need. Aspiring to live a life of radiant health? Count on confronting challenges far from that ideal, each hurdle intended to nurture faith within yourself and your body, mending imbalances along the way. This pattern extends to every longing your heart holds.

I can empathize with the ache in your heart and the frustration that lingers. I know the intensity of wanting something desperately, of wishing, praying, and surrendering to the Divine plan, trying every conceivable avenue to attract your heart's desires. The confusion sets in when, despite your efforts, the fulfillment of your desires appears delayed or distant, raising questions about its possibility. I understand this intimately because I've traversed that path repeatedly, until I unearthed a revelation—this isn't a burden to bear but a cause for celebration.

If things are taking a long time, it signifies grandness, enormity, and beauty that necessitates God's meticulous work over a substantial duration before it's ready to materialize. The more intricate the dream, the more potent the wish, the more profound the desire, the more time it demands for precise, intentional, and purposeful realization. Let it saturate, build, and grow, for the longer the wait, the bigger it'll be, the more monumental the achievement and the greater the gratitude upon its arrival.

In the waiting period, you face two choices—succumb to wallowing or embrace presence and enjoyment. I urge you to choose the latter. Revel in the in-between, for within those moments, lives are still to be lived and life is still to be savored. This moment is still your life; do you want to miss out on it, or do you want to experience it? Just because your heart's desire hasn't manifested yet doesn't mean it never will. Savor your life now, because soon, it'll be changing. Failure to appreciate your current life and self will limit the depth of your gratitude and presence, even when your desires finally materialize.

THE MORE INTRICATE
THE DREAM, THE MORE
POTENT THE WISH,
THE MORE PROFOUND
THE DESIRE, THE MORE
TIME IT DEMANDS FOR
PRECISE, INTENTIONAL,
AND PURPOSEFUL
REALIZATION.

III

Do not put limitations on God, even if today may appear as the end, or if it feels like another rock bottom, or if you feel as though you've gone backwards. Your vision might falter, unable to see the week that lies ahead, oblivious to the shifts that can drastically redefine your existence within just a few days. All you are consumed by are the previous events that brought you here, the reality of the present moment, and the worries of your potential future circumstances.

But what if, in the eyes of God, what you perceive as an end is actually a grand beginning? Perhaps this moment marks the genesis of something unprecedented, a miracle teetering on the precipice of revelation, a blessing about to flow towards you like an unstoppable tide.

You see, He can change your life instantaneously. It only takes one second to meet someone who impacts you indefinitely, to have a conversation that enlightens you, to have prosperity envelop you or to have a download that enlightens you. And so you must wake up everyday expecting the unexpected. Expect that God is working for you, not against you. Expect that blessings are unfolding, that things are turning in your favor, that prayers are being answered. Expect that everything you are seeking is being brought to you. Expect that you will be shocked by the miraculous ways He works.

Yet, within this fervent expectation, remember your role as a co-Creator with the Divine. Pursue your goals with unwavering intensity, dream expansively, and invest tirelessly in the evolution of your own being. Maintain an open heart, retool your mindset, and act in alignment with the version of yourself that has already embraced the treasures you seek.

In simple terms, if you have the privilege to wake up each day, then that means that God is yet to complete the masterpiece of your existence. If the Creator has not left you, why, then, would you abandon the limitless potential within yourself?

PERHAPS THE NUMBER
OF EXTRAORDINARY
THINGS THAT HAPPEN
TO YOU DEPENDS ON
WHAT YOU NOTICE
WITH AN OPEN HEART.

When your heart is open, you feel safe enough to ask for help. And like the meticulous hands of a divine clock-maker, God orchestrates unfathomable events to ensure you receive it.

When your heart is open, you find the courage to ask for abundance, and in response, God meticulously crafts pathways for you to bask in its overflowing riches.

When your heart is open, you feel humble enough to ask for strength. God's response is swift and unwavering, instantly fortifying you with the resilience you need to weather life's storms.

You see, when your heart embraces vulnerability, you have an unwavering faith that your desires will manifest. In this expansive state, light floods in, drawing people and opportunities towards you. You become attuned to the frequency of serendipity, the interconnected threads weaving through your existence, and the enchantment unfolding with each passing moment.

In this divine dance of openness, every encounter and every synchronicity becomes a cosmic masterpiece, a testament to the magic pulsating through the Universe at all times. And in the serene expanse of an open heart, peace finds its rightful place, settling like a gentle breeze, whispering assurances of belonging and grace.

When your heart is open, everything and anyone who is meant for you has the opportunity to flow in.

Don't give up too soon

I was driven by the boundless curiosity of what might unfold if I didn't give up. The familiarity of an unchanging life loomed as the alternative, and yet, my once-despised stubbornness emerged as a transformative force. In that unyielding determination, I unearthed a refusal to settle for my current state. My journey hadn't brought me this close only for me to halt; it was in this discontent that I embraced the challenge to dive deeper into my soul and uncover the untold possibilities that lay beyond.

I decided that I will survive long enough to experience them.

You are the 1%.

There will come a moment where vulnerability and strength intersect, and you finally find the courage to embark on a journey of self-discovery. It takes an extraordinary amount of bravery to choose a book that challenges the very foundations of your understanding, daring you to question and reshape everything you thought you knew. As you invest your precious free moments delving into the recesses of your being, seeking answers to the questions that have long eluded you, you exhibit a fearlessness that goes beyond the ordinary. It's the audacity to confront the shadows within, to unravel the complexities of your own existence.

Stepping away from the comfort of the familiar, you venture into uncharted territories where nothing feels recognizably safe. This act requires you to dissect the patterns that no longer serve your growth, to discard beliefs that were never truly yours, and to confront behaviors that hinder your alignment with your true self.

To willingly crack open your heart and let the flames of transformation consume everything you've clung to demands valor that transcends the mundane. It's a surrender to the unknown, a release of the tight grip you've maintained, embracing a future shrouded in uncertainty.

In the midst of this tumultuous journey, you find the strength to admit what no longer resonates with your soul. You bravely acknowledge the need to let go, to burn down the old and make space for the new. The urge to pray to a higher power, even if the connection feels distant, reveals a trust in something beyond your comprehension. Walking past a mirror and encountering a reflection that feels foreign demands a unique brand of determination. It's the audacity to love yourself better, to embrace the unfamiliar aspects of your evolving identity. Realizing your role in your current circumstances, without judgment, shame, or guilt requires radical honesty and acceptance with oneself.

As you choose to walk away from familiarity, from the life you've known, from the perceptions others hold of you, and from the patterns that have defined you for so long, remember this: *You are the embodiment of courage.* Even in the face of fear, uncertainty, or questioning how you arrived at this juncture, your resilience shines through. Every moment of nervousness indicates the onset of something courageous—a step into the unknown.

So, if no one has reminded you today, take pride in where you've arrived. Be proud of your courage, for even if you are scared, this moment is the prelude to doing something remarkably brave.

PART 2

UNDERSTANDING
THE SELF

She Just Can't Help But Shine

I've carried this burden well, but that doesn't mean it hasn't been heavy. Just because I'm strong enough to endure the pain, doesn't mean I've deserved it. Even though I've kept a smile on my face, there were moments when I cried just minutes before.

But you know what? Those challenges are what allowed me to become this gentle. The tough times helped me see the brighter side of all things. The aches I felt gave me the opportunity to express more compassion towards others. This gentleness, luminosity, and empathy? Well those, they're not just deserved; they've always been mine.

The tears that never flowed.

Growing up, I was shackled by the unspoken rule that negative emotions were to be buried deep within, concealed like a forbidden secret. Although laughs were embraced, smiles were celebrated and cheers were reciprocated, the lower end of the emotional spectrum was received differently. Tears were stifled, voices were hushed, and the echoes of my feelings were met with disapproval. During my childhood, I believed that vulnerability equated to weakness, that the raw pulse of my heart should be kept hidden. This wasn't done from my family members alone; they, too, were ensnared by their own unresolved distress and the whispers of external influences. Feeling heavy emotions, and I mean truly feeling, was an alien concept in the home I grew up in. We experienced things, made amends, and then immediately moved forward without processing what we just experienced.

As an adult, the struggle to untangle this emotional web haunted me. I questioned why it was so difficult for me to process and let go. And then, in a moment of revelation, I realized—I had never let out a scream in the solitude of an empty car or wept openly in the company of a friend, let alone during moments of solitude. I admired those around me who effortlessly embraced their vulnerability, shedding tears and voicing their anguish. They experienced things, processed the emotion tied to it, and then were able to move on.

A concealed part of me always held back, a dam restraining the flood of emotions. No wonder my body had been a landscape of perpetual tension, a canvas painted with every suppressed sensation, every repressed emotion. Unintentionally, I had built a fortress within, constructed from the bricks of fear, anger, resentment, and sadness, suffocating me in its heavy embrace.

Then, one day, I found myself finally standing vulnerable in front of a friend. For the first time, I surrendered to the tumult within me. It was proof that the work I had been doing on myself was working, that I no longer wanted to swallow my emotions. Tears flowed freely, words gushed forth from the depths of my chest. I was comforted, I was embraced, I was liberated. *Is this what it feels like to be human?*

That moment was a turning point—not only releasing the pent-up emotions but shattering the habit of concealing my true self. Ironically, it took adulthood to unshackle the inner child, to finally set free the captive spirit. Now, as I stand, I've granted myself permission to wield the elemental powers within, dismantling the suffocating structure I had unknowingly built. I now find solace in the cleansing downpour of all types of tears, whether in solitude or in an airport terminal surrounded by a hundred strangers, in the therapeutic dance with melancholic melodies, and in the mirror that reflects the unvarnished truth of my existence.

So, I embrace the paradox—the child within me liberated only as I crossed the threshold into adulthood.

A Silent Rage

In the tumultuous depths of your suffering, you desperately clutch your pain, a low vibration too heavy to cast upon others. It feels unjust, unfair to drag others down to your realm of despair. So, you mask your agony with politeness, covering your sorrow and suffering in a disguise of normalcy. To the world, you become an enigma of perfection—seemingly thriving, a beacon of bliss, navigating life with effortless grace. But beneath this facade, every day is a battle where your sadness simmers, unnoticed, unacknowledged, until it can no longer be contained.

Suddenly, it erupts, morphing into a fiery anger that manifests through your words, actions, and reactions. It's a storm that catches everyone off guard, especially those closest to you. Standing there, confronted by a loved one's bewildered gaze, you struggle to articulate the roots of this rage. It's not a single incident, not a momentary lapse, not their fault, but a relentless onslaught of silent trials and tribulations, each wearing you down bit by bit, like quiet whispers growing louder in a storm of anger. In this moment of raw vulnerability, you realize the enormity of your burden, a tempest too complex, too profound to be captured in mere words.

Yet, in this explosion of unbridled emotion, a silver lining emerges. This outburst, fierce as it is, becomes a catharsis—a pivotal moment where you finally acknowledge and confront the pain you've long suppressed. It's a turning point, offering a chance to delve deep within, to understand not only the roots of your pain but also the part of you that felt compelled to hide it. Over time, you begin to learn that sharing your wounds with others isn't a defeat, nor does it pull them into the depths of your despair. Instead, it becomes a powerful act of courage, an intimate bridge built between souls, reminding you that in vulnerability lies strength, and in shared struggles, we find a deeper connection and understanding.

This introspective journey, though born from turmoil, lights a path to healing and self-discovery, guiding you towards an untethered self. One that embraces and expresses emotions with the full recognition of their validity, freeing you from the shadows of restraint and leading you into the light of genuine self-expression.

The Wounded Healer

The most difficult thing I have dealt with in my life hasn't been due to external circumstances. It is my own self—a relentless interplay of mind and energy that proves both a burdensome weight and a beautiful blessing. This internal landscape is a tempest, irregular and elusive, demanding perpetual vigilance and urging me to delve deeper into its depths. It unfolds as an emotional rollercoaster, refusing predictability and keeping me on the edge of vulnerability. Yet, in this internal turbulence, I uncover the raw beauty of my humanity and the indomitable spirit that propels me forward, realizing that the most difficult battles are fought and won within the sacred chambers of my own soul, where the true essence of my strength unfolds with every heartbeat. The paradox of my existence is that none of it was random—it was written in the stars. My life as it stands, with all of its twists and turns, is exactly how God intended it to be.

In the quietude of an afternoon, I delved into the exploration of my Astrological Birth Chart, stumbling upon the revelation of my Chiron residing in the 6th House. In astrology, Chiron is often referred to as the "Wounded Healer" and is associated with our core wounds and how we can overcome them. When Chiron is placed in the 6th house of a natal chart, it can influence themes related to health, work, service, and daily routines. In that cosmic alignment, I discovered unequivocal evidence that my soul's trajectory was preordained—a destined odyssey devoted to healing, a pilgrimage that spans the realms of both physical and emotional restoration, a narrative scripted not just for myself but as a testament to the healing of others.

Chiron's placement in the 6th house weaves a poignant narrative where personal wounds and trials become a wellspring of redemption when transformed into acts of service, allowing the individual to find solace and restoration in aiding others or pursuing a helping profession. This celestial alignment hints at an intimate connection between health challenges and the journey of self-healing, steering the individual toward alternative or holistic healing modalities. The 6th house, entwined with work and daily routines, unfolds as a catalyst for personal growth, where the person discovers meaning and purpose in their professional and creative endeavors. Despite encountering trials throughout daily life, from the grind to interactions with others to health challenges, these hurdles unfurl as opportunities for transformative revelations. Anchored in a relentless pursuit of self-improvement, Chiron in the 6th house illuminates a perpetual odyssey to refine and heal, traversing the realms of health practices and personal development with a commitment to inner restoration.

An innate intuition always whispered to me that there was a deeper purpose for all of my health challenges—that each trial carried a deeper significance, that the course of my life unfolded as a deliberate design, and that the talents given to me were intended as instruments to share my accrued wisdom. Yet, the comprehension of this purpose always eluded my grasp, an enigma stretching beyond the limits of my understanding. Then, in a cosmic revelation, I stumbled upon the proof, and in that moment, I not only acknowledged but embraced the Divine truth: God had chosen me for this role in society and to be of service towards others in this way. And for that, not only do I feel inspired and empowered, but also honored to continue to fulfill His plan.

Ephesians 4:26

Throughout adulthood, I've clung to the belief that anger towards God was a sin. For years, a seething rage brewed within me, yet I suppressed it, convinced that showing hostility towards my Creator was unthinkable. How could I, surrounded by His abundant treasures and countless blessings, dare to hold fury towards the very source of my existence?

But then, one day, the dam burst. The rage that had been simmering beneath the surface could no longer be contained. My body, my soul, cried out for release—to feel the full force of that pent-up anger, to confront the pain and injustice head-on. And so, with a trembling voice and trembling heart, I dared to utter the unthinkable: *"God, how could You allow this to happen to me? Why are you doing this to your little girl?"*

The cards I'd been dealt often seemed stacked against me. The path I walked on felt like a maze of confusion and despair. Every health setback, every stumble, left me questioning my own resilience, the purpose of my struggles, and even the very existence of a higher power. Yet, amidst the turmoil, I clung to one steadfast truth: I never allowed my anger to spill over onto others. Instead, I buried it deep within, hoping to one day transmute it into something pure and radiant.

Then came the epiphany—I realized that this anger, this doubt, was not a sign of weakness or betrayal, but rather a testament to my humanity. It meant that I was alive, that I still possessed the capacity to feel and had the inclination to question. It meant that, deep down, I still believed, still yearned for answers, and still trusted in the promises of a higher power.

By allowing myself to acknowledge my anger, I found not condemnation, but redemption. It was the fiery forge where my faith was tested, tempered, and ultimately strengthened. And though the road ahead may still be fraught with trials and uncertainties, I walk it now with renewed conviction, knowing that even in my moments of doubt and despair, I am held by a love that never wavers, by a God who hears my cries and carries me through the darkest nights.

The unbearable lightness of being whole.

In the quiet moments of your independence, there emerges a subtle realization: that what once felt like a haven now carries the weight of prolonged solitude. Surrounded by love from friends, family, and a community that uplifts you, there's an undeniable warmth, yet the early morning sun, the late-night door unlocks, the soulless moments on the couch, with no echoes of another soul, footsteps walking behind you, or arms to be enveloped in breeds a question within—is this freedom or is it loneliness?

The journey leads you to a place where you build a foundation of self-love, indulging in the richness of your own company, exploring the world with joyous abandon. You become the architect of your happiness, taking yourself on dates, savoring the bliss that once eluded you. *"Look at all of the things I've done for myself and by myself,"* you proudly proclaim.

Yet, a time arrives when the echo of your solitude becomes a yearning for connection. You tire of solo adventures, empty-handed strolls through parks, and facing silent battles alone. Despite the abundant love surrounding you, the heart craves a kindred spirit, someone to share dreams with, someone to confide in, someone to lean on.

Your mind becomes a maze, seeking solace in the companionship of a soul who sees you in ways you cannot see yourself. A person who believes you are the most beautiful being in the Universe, the center of their world, the answer to their prayers. A soul who sees the raw emotions behind your smile, hears the cracks in your voice, and notices the weight on your shoulders.

The reasonable void will persist only until the day you find that connection, the one who whispers, *"It's okay, we'll get through this together,"* and shows you the light at the end of the tunnel. We were born for this level of companionship, therefore the void is warranted, but until then, you find solace in the rituals of self-love. Tucked into your bed, you embrace your own body, uttering affirmations that *'this too shall pass.'* You give yourself flowers, savor comfort food in your quiet space, and wipe your own tears. In the hushed moments of both trials and triumphs, it is your unwavering strength that cradles you, propelling you forward, and it is the resilience within you that becomes your only constant companion.

You are the one who has made you whole.

But somewhere in this dance between solitude and companionship, you begin to see you were never truly alone to begin with. In the moments of despair, your legs moved despite the heavy weight, perhaps guided by unseen Divine hands lifting you. As tears fell before the mirror, your whispered trust became a Divine pat on the back. In the random exchanges with strangers, the messages received were sent by your angels above. In the ebb and flow of life, you discover that amidst the quest for external companionship, there have always been invisible spirits lifting you. There is a consistent Divine presence assuring you that you are always protected, always held, and always safe. And maybe, just maybe, you will come to believe that you never were, and never will be, alone.

You Made Yourself a Lie

I trusted my body
Enough to know
That the painful signals it was sending
Was a sign that there was a blockage within
And I was right

I trusted my body
Enough to know
That when doctors said, *"Everything looks normal"*
I convinced them to look again
And I was right

I trusted my body
Enough to know
That the inflammation on my skin
Was a reflection of the state of my essential organs
And I was right

I trusted my body
Enough to know
Persistent sensations of swelling and nausea
Were indicative of an internal imbalance
And I was right

I trusted my body
Enough to know
The company in which it felt secure around
And which individuals triggered unease
And I was right

Yet, I never allowed my trust in my body
To stretch far enough
To embrace the logical possibility
That it holds the innate capacity to repair itself
In this, I was wrong

At what point did I get here,
Where trust halted its journey and ceased to strive
I listened to its pain, a one-sided dialogue
Neglecting the voice of its healing epilogue

To My Body:

I can turn you into poetry
Admire your disposition
Feel your heartbeat
Honor your strength
Embrace your edges
Move every inch
Take you to new places
I can stare
I can touch
I can feel
I can be
But loving you unconditionally
Still feels foreign to me

You can learn a lot from a little.

As I stood in my kitchen, engaged in the wholesome routine of preparing dinner, fate delivered an unexpected chord—the searing burn of my forearm against the hot pan. A sharp jolt raced through me, prompting an instinctive response to withdraw from the fiery grasp. My resilient body knew exactly what to do.

In the aftermath, I tended to the wounded burn, running my arm under the cold water, delicately patting it dry, and finally, covering it with a Band-Aid. In that moment, frustration flared within me—a questioning glance at the heavens, *"Really, God? Another thing to heal?"* Yet, a softer melody emanated from the depths of my higher self, whispering, *"Perhaps this is a lesson."* My intuitive mind knew what to say.

A week later, I noticed the healing composition on my forearm—it had been repaired effortlessly, tenderly, and beautifully. No external remedy had graced its surface, and yet, my skin had orchestrated its restoration without conscious orchestration. A silent knowing echoed within me, acknowledging the inherent strength of the cells in my body to mend this minor affliction.

This incident mirrored the inherent nature of a naturally healthy mind and body—doing what it's supposed to do as we navigate the rest of our lives. We've all experienced this before—minor scratches, gentle burns, fleeting bruises—and we don't lose sleep over them because we trust that our bodies have this natural knack for bouncing back. We don't stare at them, control their timeline, or fixate on when they'll heal. We just allow them to do what they're capable of doing.

Reflecting on these instances of seamless healing, where our minds effortlessly accept the possibility, begs the question: What is stopping us from believing we can bounce back from anything else? My higher self had it right; this was a lesson. The searing burn served as a reminder that the less we obsess over our challenges, the more gracefully we allow life to unfold and solve its own puzzles.

How did I get here?

I found myself in the bath one evening, clenching tightly to my legs, giving myself a warm and endearing hug that I desperately was craving from another. It was one of those moments where I just needed to be held, to be taken care of and reminded that everything will soon be okay. In that moment, something other than the water washed over me—a sense of forgiveness towards myself followed by an outpouring of tears.

For over a decade, I had resented my body. I was angry at the fact that for half of my life, living in my vessel had been a traumatic experience—where safety was a foreign concept, ease was unfamiliar and comfort was uncommon. Subconsciously, I held onto the belief that my body was not a safe space, as though it was a prison where my incarceration period was a life sentence. As I held onto myself in that bath, it felt as if, out of nowhere, the Divine voice of my higher power found expression through me. Words began to flow spontaneously, echoing in the stillness, as if guided by a force much greater than myself.

Clenching tightly to my body, I began to voice, *"I am so sorry. I am so, so sorry. I have been so cruel to you. I know you're trying to heal. I know you're doing everything you can. Please forgive me. I promise, I will learn how to love you unconditionally."*

Do you realize how tragic that is, to have to apologize to your own body and ask it for forgiveness? To notice that your emotions and thoughts have been unintentionally feeding the very suffering that it has been facing? To have to make a heart-wrenching promise for something that should be effortless and intuitive?

My journey wasn't just about forgiving my body; it extended to forgiving the part of myself that had been unconsciously molded into a form so cruel. It was a soul-deep reckoning, a moment of clarity where I saw the brutal patterns I had internalized and the urgent need to unlearn them, to heal not just the body, but the wounded spirit residing within.

I have discovered that such compassion also means forgiving myself for not knowing better. I did the best I could with the tools I had, and now as I am gathering new ones, I can do better. With each breath, I let healing fill my lungs, replacing old wounds with a resilient strength. I am more than my past, more than my pain, more than the story I kept telling myself—I am a living testament to survival and transformation.

Self-recovery leads to a destination of self-love, peace, and an unwavering belief in my own mind and body's capacity to heal itself. In this process of forgiving and loving myself, I began to not just survive; but to flourish, grounded in the understanding and acceptance of my complete self—past, present, and future.

YOUR THOUGHTS
CREATE YOUR REALITY,
SO WHICH REALITY DO
YOU WANT TO LIVE?

Your thoughts create your reality, so which reality do you want to live?

Our thoughts carry immense weight; a piece of wisdom that I repeatedly share with the people around me as I know it to be true. The veracity of this statement has guided me towards a life filled with abundance, success, and bliss, easily turning the positive thoughts into a harmonic symphony of blessings and prosperity in my physical world. But the negative thoughts have had equal weight, bringing me through a life filled with dis-ease, frustration, and a cascade of painful bodily symptoms. Despite living in a heightened state of consciousness, I couldn't help but wonder, what was I not getting, and what was I doing wrong?

Whilst in the trenches of my postoperative healing journey, I found myself on the phone with my mother, asking her how it could be that almost two months later, I was still feeling incredibly ill, as though every disease-like symptom had magically returned, despite no longer having the disease itself. I had explained that the persistent pain in my lower abdomen had not merely debilitated me; it had drastically altered my daily existence. Each effort to leave my bed became a monumental struggle, transforming the simple act of walking to my kitchen into an overwhelming challenge. Standing for any length of time became an ordeal, sapping my strength and leaving me engulfed in a massive sense of weakness. My soul yearned for freedom, to be able to live the life I wanted to live, yet my body continuously held me back from taking a single step forward. I was trapped with nowhere to go.

Upon her consolation, she posed a question, *"I'm going to say something, and I don't want you to take it the wrong way...but do you think it's all in your head?"* I now understand that this question was not a dismissal of my pain but an invitation to further explore the power of the mind-body connection, to consider the impact my present-day thoughts and emotions had on my physical well-being. But in that moment, I did take it the wrong way—I felt shattered.

How could my own mother, the one who had been a witness to every challenge I faced, the sole confidante of my often-dismissed struggles with doctors, and my steadfast companion through countless appointments, tests, and procedures since I was twelve years old, suggest that my suffering was merely a figment of my imagination?

Yet, I knew that if there was no truth in her words, they wouldn't have triggered me so deeply. But they pierced my very soul, stinging a raw nerve and forcing me to reevaluate my self-perception. In that instance of painful introspection, I realized the potential validity in her inquiry, a truth I would have otherwise confidently dismissed.

I became aware of how I've consistently placed enormous pressure on myself, driven solely by a desire to prove that I can accomplish, become, and heal anything. This self-imposed determination, once my greatest strength, morphed into excessively high expectations for myself. Each time I failed to meet these self-imposed and unrealistic deadlines for success and healing, I felt a sense of defeat. I was perpetually pushing myself to reach stages I wasn't yet prepared for, caught in a cycle of expectation and disappointment.

Her question, initially a crushing blow, transformed into a gateway towards freedom. It shined a light on the fact that the emotional strain I was imposing on myself extended beyond my psyche. It manifested physically, rendering the lower part of my body rigid and unresponsive. My legs were seized in numbness with each attempt to move, and my digestive system froze. Unknowingly, I had projected my inner turmoil of feeling constrained, overwhelmed, and stressed into my very physiology, affecting how my body operated and perceived pain. During this time, I ran multiple tests to check the state of my body. And for the first time in many years, my test results came back balanced, clear, and normal. *My mother was right, and I had data to prove it.*

Breaking free from a sensation long unnoticed is an immense challenge. How does one release the grip of self-inflicted pressure and allow it to dissolve? I was clinging desperately to my traumatic past, unable to process and release a decade worth of emotions, sometimes even unaware of what I was exactly trying to release. Yet, this very consciousness, recognizing that my mindset was fueling symptoms akin to disease, spurred a transformative shift in my behavior, as I no longer wanted to live in this way. I *couldn't* live this way.

Whenever negative thoughts surfaced, I chose a different approach: I paused, observed them without judgment, and instead of nurturing these thoughts, I gently reminded myself, *"I choose to let this pass."* This simple, yet powerful mantra became a tool for liberation, guiding me towards emotional release and healing. I began to digest what I was feeling, allowing those emotions to flow through me, rather than remaining stagnant within.

Gradually, this affirmation wove itself into the fabric of my daily life. It was not just about letting things pass; it was about consciously *choosing* to let them pass. I began to selectively nurture certain thoughts while gently releasing others. This process brought a striking realization: my thoughts had been overwhelmingly focused on my health and physical state, overshadowing thoughts about my passions, interests, and what truly brought me joy. This shift in perspective marked a significant step towards a more balanced and fulfilling mindset.

My mind transformed from a burden into a sanctuary, a peaceful realm where I no longer felt the need to escape. Over the course of a few months, the self-inflicted pressure dissolved, and my body became liberated from no longer being constrained. My nurturing thoughts created a new reality—one where my body was beginning to feel more at ease, slowly feeling safe enough to heal as it was always designed to.

Hero

I prided myself on my emotional intelligence and the level of vulnerability I was open to, yet when I stood in front of him, the man who held the keys to my heart, I couldn't even tell him how much love I held for him. The fear of rejection took over me, forcing me to be paralyzed in my words, only allowing me to express surface level remarks that didn't even remotely express what I was trying to really say. That's when I discovered—I still have work to do. I must first understand the barriers within me that hold me back from expressing love, in order to break the barriers outside of me that prevent me from receiving love. Therein laid the gates towards freedom.

Being aware that I was the one preventing myself from attracting what I desired gave me the opportunity to look inwards with curiosity. How can I expect to foster a soul-fulling, unconditional, passionate, and romantic love, if I was not only unable to express myself fully but also validate with myself what I was feeling? I knew this was critical in order to open the door towards that level of human connection, yet I continuously held myself back from admitting the sensations in my soul.

Once I felt curious about my limitations, I began to question my choices. What is preventing me from speaking my truth? What wounds have I yet to heal? Is it fear of this chapter closing permanently? I no longer felt comfortable in that space without self-allowance, so I started to choose differently, allowing my actions to be altered. I decided to let go of the "what-ifs" in an effort to gain inner peace. Once I began to change behavior, those small steps towards liberation eventually led me to a path filled with precious moments where my vulnerability shined, where my fears diminished and where my truth stood. I not only dissolved the blocks within me but also gave him the opportunity to do the same.

That's the beauty in healing parts of yourself—it may first be individualistic, but the lasting effect trickles down towards the people around you and fosters a chain reaction of self-actualization. To have enough strength and resilience to crack yourself open with no expectations on what lies ahead, you are able to facilitate a domino effect of transformation through your own healing—one that others will silently hold you accountable for.

This is what makes you a hero.

Parenting Your Potential

There is a parent within each of us—a voice that exudes tranquility, strength, unwavering compassion, and boundless resources. This voice is often heard as an echo in the far distance, whispers of profound truths that we, regrettably, tend to overlook. Instead, we all too readily listen to the demands of our inner fears, anxieties, worries, and frustrations, as if they were comfortable old friends. We find solace in feeding the predictable, even if it means neglecting the nurturing thoughts that could uplift, console, and fortify us. We cling to what is known, fearing the uncertain, even though the other side holds the potential for growth and transformation.

Yet, a relentless cycle ensues—a parade of similar days, where your eyes are filled with burning tears and a shattered heart permeates with numbness. You may beg, *"How much more can I take?"* In those moments, the parent within you speaks softly but resolutely, *"You are safe. You are okay. You are loved. You are kind. You are beautiful. You are strong. You can handle this. You can handle anything. This too shall pass."*

Your irrational mind, however, persistently counters, *"Are you sure?"* It becomes a battle of two voices—one born from a version of yourself conditioned to embrace doubt and the other, the parent within, which knows your deepest truths.

The challenge becomes evident—being aware that a rational, composed, fearless, empathetic, and capable aspect of your being exists should naturally lead you to embody it fully. And so you must make the conscious choice to not neglect this inner parent and instead, amplify its voice, so that its wisdom guides your actions. You'll begin to unlock the door to a life of limitless empowerment and leave behind restricted belief systems.

The parent within you holds the keys to your liberation, and all you need to do is shed the heavy armor of doubt, trusting its capability and allowing it to lead you toward your most authentic and empowered self.

Nostalgic for a time that never existed.

The magic of nostalgia lies in its ability to transport us to a time when life seemed lighter, when every song had a story, and every friend was a companion in the grand adventure of youth. We trace the lines of our lives through the pages of a book, feeling the echoes of emotions that once shaped us. Old photographs with our parents become portals to an era where love was simple, and the weight of the world was a distant thought.

Yet, amidst the euphoria of reminiscence, a poignant truth surfaces—nostalgia, our selective curator of memories, tends to decorate the past with hues of rapture, filtering out the storms that raged in the background. Love, laughs, cheers, hugs, and smiles dominate the canvas of recollection, while the trials and the tempests fade to the periphery.

In this realization, we confront the paradox of our own minds. Why do we cling to the sunlit fragments while conveniently forgetting the shadows that lent depth to our past? Some of our favorite songs once played against the backdrop of heartbreak. The friend we now miss resides in the shadows of betrayal due to wrongs committed many times over. The film that comforted us was a lifeline in times of distress and the book that fell into our lap did so amidst the chaos of confusion. That photograph? It captured a moment frozen in time, concealing the storm that raged just moments before the shutter clicked.

And so, the lesson unfolds like the pages of a well-worn novel—the past, for all its allure, was not a utopia.

Pain, fear, loneliness, anger, and confusion were still part of our yesteryears, intermingling with the joy, forming a symphony of complexity. Now, as we stand on the precipice of our present, we must be reminded that as we delve into the sanctuary of our memories, we must do so with open eyes and honest hearts. Yes, we can relish the past, but let's not forget its shadows. We can reminisce, but let's do so with the wisdom that hindsight brings. We can reflect, but let's do so with an unwavering commitment to truth.

For, in the midst of our longing for the past, we must acknowledge that we are here, in the present, navigating new storms and seeking breaks of sunshine. It's tempting to imagine that the past was an idyllic paradise, but the reality is, it never truly was. And, we're no longer there. Within this moment, the challenges may persist, the pain may linger, and confusion may envelop us, yet so does the potential for joy, bliss, and peace.

So, let us not be confined to the sepia-toned illusions of the past. We stand in a moment that will one day be a future version of nostalgia. If we can envision ourselves looking back and saying, *"Life was so much better back then,"* which we most likely will, then let's make sure there is truth to that statement. Let's infuse this very moment with meaning, embracing both the struggles and the triumphs, for in life, the storm and the sunshine coexist.

Paradise

You'll begin to reflect on the pinnacle moments of your life, those instances where you felt pure rapture and an ungodly type of euphoria that suffused your entire body. The level of consciousness you can't fully articulate using words; the type of bliss that only Schedule 1 drugs can supposedly provide. Yet for you, it sprang from the depths of your soul—the purity that God had intentionally designed you with.

When you recall those joyful moments, remembering the laughs you shared, the words you spoke, and the cherished faces around you, you start to wonder... knowing your heart has known it, lived it, thrived in it, why would you ever doubt its return?

I hope you understand that such paradise isn't a fleeting guest in the home of your heart, but the very foundation it's built upon. The pursuit of happiness is not a chase; it's a return—to the essence of your being, where every heartbeat is an echo of infinite bliss. This is the homecoming you must embrace.

Reflect, recreate, repeat.

Take note of those moments you felt the most alive. Notice those souls whose presence emanated such potent energy that it stirred your very core. Recall individuals with whom you engaged in profound dialogues, unveiling the secrets hidden in the depths of your psyche. Reflect on those actions that rekindled the fearless, unburdened essence of your younger self—free from fear, guilt, or shame. Consider the places you've ventured, where awe and wonder enveloped you and bridged you to universal unity. Embrace those daily habits that call upon your inner strength, a part of you that's sometimes hidden beneath life's demands. Reflect, recreate, repeat. That's how you alchemize and become your authentic self, day by day.

Conscious Creation

Do you know what's magical? At a distinct moment in time, God intentionally decided, *"The world is in need of their unique spirit."* He chose to place you in a specific family, bless you with your parents, and root you within a nurturing community. He guided your path to attend the right school, pursue the fulfilling job, and reside in a city that would shape your journey. He lovingly curated your circle of friends and crafted a tapestry of experiences, all to mold you into the person you are meant to be. He intentionally gave you a unique gift, one where your creativity can impact the lives of others. Because it is through you—through the vibrancy of your energy, the brilliance of your mind, and the depth of your heart, through your victories and the resilience in your challenges, through your journey of overcoming—that the world will witness and experience a living testament of God's boundless and unfailing goodness.

Your existence is not mere chance; it's a deliberate and meticulously crafted masterpiece. You are here for a reason, playing an essential role in this lifetime, destined to leave a permanent mark on the world.

YOUR EXISTENCE IS
NOT MERE CHANCE;
IT'S A DELIBERATE
AND METICULOUSLY
CRAFTED MASTERPIECE.

This is a story of how two strangers forever
altered my perception in the miraculous ways
God and your guardian angels work.

In July 2023, amidst the vibrant buzz of an Atlanta hotel lobby, hours before my destined return to New Jersey, destiny whispered through an unexpected twist. A sudden notification from my airline confirmed a delayed departure, sparking a flash of irritation within me. Yet, it was in this moment of uncertainty that my colleague suggested a flight change that could alter my path. Standing at this crossroads, I contemplated the ease of transition versus the allure of the unknown, which ultimately led me to reach out to the airline with a hopeful heart.

As I navigated the complexities of changing flights, a serendipitous discovery emerged—my flight number, DL2226, resonated with a deeper meaning, a sign from the Universe affirming I was exactly where I needed to be. This revelation, a clear message from my inner wisdom, urged me to embrace my original journey. And when the airline's process proved more cumbersome by requiring third-party intervention, it was the final, resounding confirmation—I chose to trust the plan laid out for me, embracing the unexpected delay as part of a grander design, a testament to my belief that sometimes, the Universe conspires in mysterious ways to guide us on our true path.

As I walked through Atlanta International Airport, a wave of wonder washed over me, sparking a flow of intriguing questions. What adventures lay ahead? Who would cross my path and what enlightening conversations might unfold? Could a chance encounter with someone from my past be in the cards? Is this the day I meet the love of my life? This curiosity allowed me to embrace the moment with an open heart, as I was keenly aware that the path ahead promised transformative experiences beyond my current comprehension.

An hour later, I luckily received another flight notification that my departure time was back to its original programming. So, I began wandering towards my gate to search for a seat where my eyes would be wide open. I initially chose to sit in the middle section of the gate, far away from the windows and most people, yet a few seconds after I propped my belongings, my intuitive voice urged me to move there—an open seat next to a woman sitting by the window.

Initially, I overlooked this woman as she seemed worlds apart from me, her age and aura painting a life story vastly different from my own. Seated beside her, lost in her own Universe watching a film on her phone, I found myself absorbed in people-watching as they converged at the gate.

Then, an older man approached, his presence a vivid testament to life's trials and resilience. His singular eye, the limp in his step, the scars etching stories of survival on his face, and the staples in his head spoke of a journey marked by many challenges, mirroring aspects of my own. In that moment, a wave of empathy washed over me. Silently and without his knowing, I sent him thoughts of kindness, a quiet acknowledgment of our shared resilience in the face of life's trials.

This man, a figure of strength and mystery, settled into the seat originally meant for me, right across from where I sat. I watched him, intrigued by his actions and the quiet dignity with which he arranged his belongings. There was a subtle yet compelling curiosity in me about the chapters of life he had lived through. Then, almost as if guided by an unseen force, he looked up and our eyes met, where in that brief exchange of glances, a connection was formed. We shared a smile, a simple yet powerful gesture of mutual recognition and unspoken understanding that bridged our worlds for what I originally thought would only be a moment.

As our plane stood ready at the gate, a collective sense of anticipation filled the air. However, an announcement from our pilot about a malfunction in the plane's ventilation system momentarily paused our departure. While some passengers expressed frustration, I found myself embracing the unexpected gift of time, curious about the opportunities this extra hour might bring.

The woman beside me, initially a stranger of contrasting experiences, initiated a conversation that shifted the atmosphere. In regards to the passengers who began showing their anger, she looked towards me and expressed, *"I don't understand why people do that, it's not the Pilot's fault! And where do you have to be that is so important? I wish people would be kinder and more patient."* It was at that moment I discovered that this woman, who originally felt very diverse from me, actually shared a similar mindset. We began a deeper conversation, where I learned how she was on her own spiritual awakening, longing for a life filled with more love, peace, and kindness.

I then posed a question, knowing she would relate to the place I was coming from: *"I'm not sure where you stand in terms of religion and spirituality, but do you believe in angel numbers?"* After she responded with a resounding 'yes', the door opened towards a deeper conversation. *"Well, I'm not sure if you noticed,"* I excitedly shared, *"But our flight number is DL2226, and '222' means we're at the right place, at the right time. I'm not sure why we're all here, but I have a feeling something great is going to happen."* She smiled and agreed, now also feeling the excitement of what lies ahead. *"Let's stay tuned and find out!"*

As we exchanged life stories, discussing our reasons

for traveling to New Jersey, our backgrounds, and careers, she shared her work in the healthcare industry in Atlanta. This led me to open up about my own health journey, marked by challenges and misdiagnoses, and how it taught me the importance of self-advocacy. *"My whole health journey has been filled with doctors never believing my word, and always suggesting that the pain and discomfort we're all in my head,"* I explained. Her insights into healthcare malpractice added depth to our conversation, highlighting the shared understanding that sometimes, the most needed connections are forged in the most unexpected places and situations.

Her curiosity led her to ask for more details on my health, where I opened up about my battle with Endometriosis, a relentless condition that had been the unseen force behind my chronic pelvic pain, gut issues, hypothyroidism, vitamin deficiency, hormonal imbalances, chronic fatigue, and more. It serendipitously turned out that this woman was not just a listener but an expert on Endometriosis. She offered not just sympathy but valuable insights into the disease, discussing its underlying causes and pathways to healing with a depth of understanding that was both surprising and enlightening.

Remarkably, she proposed connecting me with one of her clients, the top Endometriosis specialist in the United States who was located in Atlanta, known for his expertise in excision surgery. While I expressed my heartfelt thanks for this incredible offer, I shared that I had already undergone the surgery two months earlier with a great specialist in my area. However, the path to recovery had been riddled with doubts and questions about its effectiveness. Her offer, knowledge, and the unexpected alignment of her expertise with my struggles not only empowered me but also reignited a sense of hope and possibility. In our unfolding dialogue, she gently probed about my current symptoms where I candidly shared that my post-surgery experiences—pelvic pressure, sciatic pain, chronic bloating, painful menstrual cycles, and so much more—mirrored those I had before the operation. I explained how while there was initial improvement, it felt as if I had gone backwards. This resulted in confusion and despair creeping back in, casting doubts on my body's ability to heal and function as God designed it to.

I recounted personal anecdotes and the Divine signals that had guided me prior to the surgery. I shared how it was by spiritually connecting with my late grandmother that I learned that the underlying cause of all health struggles was from Endometriosis. A week after, I conducted an ultrasound that proved her message to be right. I prayed to my grandmother each day, asking her to guide me on this path and show me where to go and explore what needed to be explored. The recurring appearance of '444', a number I associated with Divine protection and a heartfelt connection to her, had been a beacon in the weeks leading to the discovery of my surgeon and the surgery itself. Deep down, I believed the operation was the right step towards healing, yet my mind wrestled with opposing thoughts, questioning its success and my body's capacity to recover. *"I don't know what to believe or think or do anymore,"* I admitted.

When I mentioned '444', this woman's expression shifted dramatically, as if I had unveiled a profound truth. This was the moment where I felt an overwhelming sense of Divine presence, not just spiritually but tangibly in my reality. She reached out, placing her hand on my lap, and said with a deep sense of connection, *"Love, this is why we're here today. The moment you spoke of 444, I knew your grandmother's spirit is with us. My home address is also 444, a synchronicity too random to ignore. What I want you to understand from this is that your intuition is right. Your surgery was a success. It was your grandmother's guiding hand that led you to this path. Embrace our encounter as an affirmation of your journey towards healing. Be gentle with yourself and your body. The road you've traveled, filled with challenges and trauma, has been filled with immense courage. Trust in your body's ability to heal, believe in the process, and know that you will indeed find wellness and strength."*

This revelation marked a transformative moment, a clear sign that our meeting was more than coincidence, a Divine orchestration that bridged the spiritual and physical realms, affirming the presence and guidance of loved ones beyond.

I expressed my deepest gratitude to this woman, a thankfulness that resonated from the core of my being, more profound than any I had ever known. Her words and insights had shifted my perspective, illuminating my understanding of healing, the resilience of my body, and the intricate mosaic of life—not just in the physical world but the ethereal, too. Her presence and guidance were a beacon of hope, transforming my outlook and empowering me to see my journey through a lens of renewed faith, pride and possibility.

As the hour drew to a close and boarding commenced, our paths diverged, never to cross again. Settled into the window seat of the plane, I gazed out to the tarmac radiating with sunshine, a sight so serene it seemed to speak directly to my soul. In that moment, my heart was enveloped in an unprecedented sense of peace, like a long, deep exhale. It was a moment of deep trust in the Divine plan, a surrender to the wisdom of God's work. This encounter had taught me to accept where I stood in life's journey, to trust and even embrace the challenges I faced. It was an affirmation to walk through the storm with faith, recognizing that each step was guided by a higher purpose and leading me toward deeper healing and understanding.

Shortly thereafter, I ventured towards the bathroom and there he was again—the man with whom I had shared a brief but memorable exchange of smiles earlier. He was arranging his belongings in the overhead compartment and as I got closer to his row, he settled into his seat, offering another warm smile but this time accompanied by a friendly wave. With the newfound bliss and peace resonating in my heart, I mirrored his gesture, returning a smile filled with the same warmth and kindness. As I passed by, I offered a sincere wish, *"Have a good flight!"* It was a small but meaningful expression that stood as proof that even the briefest human interactions can leave an impact.

During those next two hours, somewhere in between Atlanta and New Jersey, I found myself immersed in deep introspection. The day's events had unveiled new layers of my being—a heightened awareness of my surroundings, a keen observation of the souls around me, the mindful presence I embodied, the inherent kindness in my actions, and the openness in my heart. There was a sense of pride that welled up in me—pride in my innate curiosity, in viewing life's unexpected turns as hidden treasures, in initiating conversations with those unknown, and in radiating warmth through simple gestures.

My thoughts then turned to the broader significance of the day's encounters. The woman had undoubtedly left a permanent mark on my life, but what about the man with whom I had shared a heartfelt exchange? I simmered in that question for a bit, until a clear and truthful realization dawned on me: I had seen this man not just with my eyes but with my soul, recognizing him as a kindred spirit amidst a world that might often overlook or misunderstand him. In our brief interaction, I had become a source of light in his day—a stranger who not only noticed him but also genuinely embraced his presence. The role that woman played for me was the role I played for this man. This revelation highlighted the power of human connection and empathy, where even slight acts of recognition can be a lasting gift to another.

Now, in this moment, I find myself at a crossroads of perception—where the mundane intertwines with the profound, where meaning resides in both the nothing and the everything. You might have read through my story and wondered if I was a desperate seeker architecting my own guidance, and whether these occurrences were mere coincidences and far from Divine.

However, I will forever embrace this experience as nothing short of a supernatural, Divinely orchestrated gift. It served as a luminous reminder that our higher powers are at work for us in ways beyond our comprehension, answering our prayers in a subtle manner, weaving a tapestry where we are all deeply interconnected. This experience clarified that every moment holds the potential for magic, that every encounter, every twist of fate, is a chance to witness the extraordinary in the ordinary.

I urge you to embrace the two core lessons from this experience: the first truth being that everything in life is unfolding for your benefit, not against you. Despite the confusion I had felt during this time and the yearning in my heart to officially bring this painful journey to a close, it was after this very moment where my heart lastingly opened up, my faith permanently deepened and I eternally embodied absolute surrender. The second truth is that love is a pervasive force, ever-present in and around us, often manifesting in the most unexpected places and experiences. Every moment is a chance to radiate love, whether through words, deeds, or silent thoughts, and so we must always choose to let the warmth of our hearts illuminate the world around us, and to never let anything or anyone allow us to close it. These perspectives are a powerful shift, inviting you to see each event, challenge, and encounter as a tailored opportunity for growth, connection and learning.

After this life-changing encounter, my path to healing transformed, becoming a journey marked by patience, curiosity, and grace instead of control, fear, and anger. While my physical transformation would still challengingly unfold for months after, I began to release the self-inflicted pressure of adhering to an arbitrary timeline. Anytime I'd find myself resorting to old thought patterns, I'd remind myself of this experience. Over time, the doubts about my surgery's effectiveness dissolved, replaced by a deep trust in the Divine plan. Embracing this journey with an open and peaceful heart, I surrendered to the wisdom of a higher power, confident in the belief that every day, despite what it held, would bring me closer towards healing and wholeness, and ultimately towards the resilient woman I am destined to be, strong and unyielding in the face of any of life's challenges.

To the remarkable man whose name remains a mystery, and to the lovely Mrs. Wilson, your influence has been unforgettable. Your brief presence in my life has etched a permanent, cherished place in my heart, and now, hopefully in the hearts of others. I am eternally grateful that you have given me the ability to witness, experience and feel God's eternal love. If this book has made its way into your hands, my deepest wish is for both of you to experience a journey filled with boundless joy, peace, and fulfillment. May God's grace continually envelop you, offering protection and comfort, as a perpetual reminder of the love and light you've shared with the world.

Oyster

Worry is believing that God won't get it right, stress is believing that what happened in the past will manifest in the future, and control is believing that nothing will change unless we put in a lot of effort. But what if we switched the strategy?

Perhaps we turn our worries into faith, trusting that things will always work out in the end. Perhaps we turn our stressors into relaxation, trusting that we always have an opportunity to download wisdom. Perhaps we turn our need to control into surrender, trusting that God can do more when we open the playing field.

In faith, relaxation, and surrender, we find our true strength, discovering that when we let go, we don't ever lose—we gain a Universe filled with opportunities and experiences that further enlighten us.

Agape

Every sunset unveils a masterpiece in the sky, a canvas of hues that never fail to leave you breathless. Each time, you declare it as the most enchanting spectacle ever witnessed. The vivid colors, the gentle rays, the powerful warmth all create a scene that etches itself into your soul. Yet, as you stand mesmerized, a few days later a new sunset emerges, brighter, lighter, and different, erasing the memory of all that came before. In those moments, the magic of the past sunsets pales in comparison, though they were once your most magical, beautiful, and captivating visuals.

Such is the essence of life. When you experience a remarkable moment, it becomes the pinnacle of joy, the epitome of rapture, the embodiment of ultimate freedom. It sets a standard that seems insurmountable. Yet, life surprises you, unfolding experiences far greater than what you once held dear. The joy deepens, the feeling of being alive intensifies, and a sense of peace settles within. *"It can't get better than this,"* you tell yourself, only to discover that it does. Even if current circumstances may not match the heights of your past, there is still life to be embraced, created and nurtured. Make sure to hold it all before your standard is set higher.

Passage

When God gives you a nudge to do something—do it. No matter how grand or minimal it may seem, the intuitive pull is the action that He has sent deliberately for you to take. What lies on the other side of it is irrelevant, for who you become afterwards is the ultimate purpose. It is the character development that He is building.

It may seem incredibly small—offering a compliment to someone you pass by, choosing to invite someone distant to a gathering you're hosting, signing up to a workout class that seems challenging, listening to a podcast that feels intriguing, researching a career path you're exploring, saying 'Hi,' to a stranger you're enamored with, reaching out to a friend you haven't connected with recently, walking into a store that draws you in, or taking the first step towards fulfilling a dream. The list is endless and the possibilities are infinite.

Within those actions, something within you changes. Your heart feels a shift, your mind is expanded, your body is strengthened, or your soul is nourished. It's as though that small action, whether it was intentional, intuitive, or accidental, was quietly leading you to the answer to a prayer you've been whispering.

In essence, to attract better, you must become better. You can't repeat the same decisions and expect a different outcome. You can't take the same actions and yield new results. The only way to evolve your life is to alter the actions you take at every present moment. Through each shift in behavior, you are setting a new path for yourself. You allow yourself to meet new people, foster new experiences, encounter new emotions, discover new wisdom, and witness new heights. What once started as a silent nudge, becomes the foundation of a new destiny.

Because over time, those nudges transform from minor prompts to a way of being. Once you begin operating from your intuitive state, your character transforms from what you've known to who you've wanted to become. Your hunger and thirst for a vibrant life no longer is a mere wish that will be fulfilled in the distant future, but instead, the way in which you live at every moment.

Come up for air

Rivers bravely remind us that beautiful things exist in both serenity and chaos. Even when there are twists and turns, the water still trusts that it has ample space to freely move. Even if there is a blockage from a rock or a broken branch, the water allows itself to pivot and tread towards a new direction. Although the elemental force is noticed during the light, its presence is still heard in the midst of darkness, through every ripple and splash. In areas with changes in elevation, we find that the individual molecules persevere in strength through their collective effort. In moments during a rainfall, the water moves with more intensity, sounding more forceful and louder. In moments of brisk sunshine and low wind, it moves with effortless grace from a place of calmness and serenity. Although the elemental force is highly influenced by the environment in which it traverses—it serves as a beautiful reminder that despite what comes its way, it continues to allow itself to proceed wherever it is being guided.

Perhaps we can see ourselves in the same light—that regardless of what the external conditions are and the barriers that are laid before us, we, too, can beautifully flow in the direction that God is guiding us toward.

I CONSOLE MY INNER CHILD
AND TELL HER, *IT'S OKAY.*
I LOOK AT MY CURRENT
SELF IN THE MIRROR AND
TELL HER, *IT'S STILL OKAY.*

Every current pattern in your life was born from a series of adaptations, a response to the experiences that shaped you all to keep your body safe at some point in time. Reflect for a moment on the intricate patterns that define your existence—the routines, habits, and idiosyncrasies that have become your essence. Cast your mind back to a time before these patterns took root, and imagine explaining your current reality to a younger self. Would they recognize the person you've become? Would they comprehend the journey that led you here?

In my own life, there are patterns that seem unfathomable, born from health struggles that spanned a decade. Take, for instance, the crippling anxiety that accompanies travel. Despite an innate love for exploration, the specter of illness loomed large, casting a shadow over every journey. The mere thought of navigating unfamiliar environments filled me with dread: What if sickness struck? How would I cope with dietary restrictions? How could I maintain a façade of normalcy around others amidst the turmoil?

For me, using unfamiliar restrooms in foreign places always triggered anxiety for me. If I couldn't find one or didn't feel comfortable whilst using it, the resulting physical discomfort would cast a shadow over my entire day, souring the joy of travel. Countless family trips were marred by my health struggles, forcing us to cancel plans and confine ourselves to the hotel room. That's when the heavy burden of guilt began for spoiling the experiences of those around me. So, as I transitioned into young adulthood and ventured on trips with friends, I adopted a different approach. Instead of burdening them with my setbacks, I encouraged them to continue without me. Though I shed the weight of guilt, a sense of emptiness and longing plagued my heart as I missed out on cherished moments.

In response, I forged a litany of precautions and rituals, each layer of defense to protect myself. What began as a modest assortment of remedies grew into a real arsenal, a survival kit customized to endure times of uncertainty. Every aspect of travel—from accommodation to amenities—was scrutinized with a meticulousness bordering on obsession.

If I could confront my younger self, standing on the precipice of these trials, I'd struggle to articulate how I arrived where I am. The genesis of these patterns is beyond me, lost amid the ebb and flow of circumstance. Yet, I'd convey a simple truth: every trial and every tribulation compelled me to adapt—to evolve—in pursuit of safety and solace.

But here's the crux: we can adapt for the better. In the pursuit of safety and solace, we possess the power to redefine ourselves, to chart a new course unburdened by the shackles of the past. It begins with a single choice— a departure from the familiar, a leap into the unknown. Each decision carries the potential for transformation, each divergence a step toward a brighter tomorrow.

So instead of harboring shame, embarrassment, or guilt about where I find myself today, I've learned to offer myself compassion. It's all okay—the struggles, the adaptations, the journey. Each challenge compelled me to adapt and survive, shaping me into who I am today. But now, I can choose to adapt in ways that break old patterns no longer serving me, to find safety in new, empowering ways.

One day, I'll see the light

Unseen hours, silent battles
Tearful showers, a mind that devours
Yet I still rise, from the darkest shadows
As I explore the depths of my being
I'm lead to self-healing
Guided by the stars
A beacon so bright
Hidden in plain sight
I ignite my own light

PART 3

HONORING
THE SELF

Unrecognizable Figure

In order to honor your entire self, you must not resent the experiences that sculpted you into the person that you now are. If those moments were stripped from your story, who would you stand as in this present moment? Diminished in empathy? Inflated with judgment? Depleted in generosity? Filled with pessimism? Deprived of awareness?

It is not the experiences themselves that warrant thankfulness, but the growth they seed within you, the wisdom embedded into your very soul and the insights uniquely cultivated from these encounters. For these are the treasures that cannot be unearthed anywhere else.

Over time, the healing adds up.

Healing is like navigating a vast and intricate jigsaw puzzle. We have no idea where to begin, just that we know we have to. Each piece, irregular and unique, represents a fragment of our journey towards wholeness. It requires unwavering focus and unyielding determination to delicately interlock these disparate parts, crafting a mosaic of our resilience and growth.

Yet, amidst the tangled complexity of our healing journey, we fixate on the elusive final image. We yearn to grasp its entirety, to glean all insights in one swift revelation. But healing, we come to realize, is not a destination reached in a single leap. It's a painstaking process, where each piece is forged with tender care, gradually evolving from one to hundreds, each a precious repository of wisdom.

With every revelation, another piece of the puzzle falls into place, illuminating the intricate connections between our experiences. And sometimes, we have to go back to the start and rethink our strategy, undoing certain pieces to find their true place. But through understanding the dimensions and shapes of our journey, we eventually discern where each piece fits, composing together a snapshot of our transformation.

Though the grand design may remain shrouded in mystery, there comes a sense of anticipation and excitement as we glimpse the foundation of our healing masterpiece. In that moment, the once-daunting puzzle transforms from a source of confusion into a beacon of certainty, guiding us towards the revelation awaiting just beyond the horizon.

Forgiveness

The biggest lie whispered into the ears of our youth is the notion that growing up means becoming impervious to life's tribulations. We were handed the script that with each passing chapter, our minds would evolve into fortresses capable of withstanding any storm. Yet, here we stand, in the pulsating beat of our late twenties, thirties, forties, and so forth, still feeling the echoes of wounds etched at eight, twelve, or eighteen.

Throughout life, there will be days where all you crave is your mother's comforting voice. Moments will arise that test the very limits of our resilience, urging us to release torrents of emotion through an outpouring of tears. We'll discover an inner longing to unleash a primal scream or gaze into the abyss of a wall, yet as adults, there's a pervasive sense that such raw expressions and desires are forbidden to us.

The difference, however, is that as we age, we have the armor of wisdom, enlightenment, and a toolbox filled with the instruments of experience. Will anger revisit? Unquestionably, for we are human. Will fear linger in the corridors of our minds? Beyond question, for we are human. Will the specter of loneliness weave its threads around our hearts? Without a doubt, for we are human.

Every moment and each emotion is a new encounter, a sacred journey into the uncharted territories of the evolving self. What once cut deep may cut again, but the blade has evolved. The melody of emotions will echo, but the instruments may have changed. The storms will revisit, but the cast of shadows will be different. However, we hold the key to how we react to these novel experiences.

As the chapters of life unfold, we author a narrative imbued with the ink of growth. Will we make more educated decisions? Absolutely, for we have grown. Will we be more discerning in who we give our precious energy to? Undoubtedly, for we have grown. Will we dissect the origins of those disquieting emotions? Without question, for we have grown.

Accept the chaos, for within it lies the crucible of your evolution. Be kind to the traveler that is you, navigating uncharted waters—you've never been here before in this exact way. Let self-compassion be the compass that guides you through the tumultuous seas of existence. In your unfolding saga, remember: you cannot heal a mind or body that you resent.

ACCEPT THE CHAOS,
FOR WITHIN IT LIES
THE CRUCIBLE OF
YOUR EVOLUTION.

Human Nature

Why is it that we readily commend our past selves, yet struggle to extend the same depth of love to the person we are in this very moment? Is there no cause for celebration, a recognition of the efforts, achievements, and growth that encapsulate our present? Surely, as time unfolds, we will look back upon this juncture with the same admiration, feeling a sense of pride and fulfillment for all we navigated during this season of our lives. We'll find a photograph from this moment in time or a written journal entry and express, *"I'm so proud of my past self for all that they did."*

The paradox lies in our ability to envision our future selves—those who conquer monumental goals, attain financial freedom, radiate vitality, explore the world, nurture families, find purpose, and serve others. We already bask in pride for these imagined versions, marveling at their accomplishments with a sense of awe and wonder. Yet, unwittingly, we lend our pride to a future state, postponing the gratification we could experience in the here and now.

There is certainly enough cause for celebration. Goals partially achieved are stepping stones on the path to fulfillment. Every venture into different career paths propels us toward our destined purpose. The commitment to enhancing our well-being is a worthy investment of our time and energy. Establishing boundaries while navigating the world is the courageous journey toward forging meaningful connections.

Why postpone self-regard until everything aligns perfectly? The truth is, we're in a constant state of evolution, and waiting for an ideal future may mean missing the richness of the present. The uncertainty of tomorrow and the unpredictability of our journey through life urge us to question: Do we wish to persist in a life devoid of personal fulfillment, never acknowledging the value we hold within ourselves at this stage? What is truly stopping us from commemorating all that we currently are?

New Normal

In the space between your past self and your future self, there must come a time of radical acceptance. There will always be more to do and more to heal, but to release yourself from the fight, you must acknowledge what was, honor the progress that's been made and accept what the now holds. Forge a path to integrate it seamlessly into your existence without forcing entry into your next phase.

Because the reality is, not everything can manifest instantaneously; some things must unfold organically over time. Yet, there are daily actions you can partake in that can skillfully bridge the gap. Notice the difference between over-exerting yourself and simply existing. This balance, in itself, becomes the art of mindful navigation.

**Don't disregard the slight actions that can lead
to grand changes in your state of being.**

Everything will work out. And until it does, or until you can see it, take care of yourself—mind, body, and spirit. Take a warm bath. Breathe in fresh air. Observe the diverse people walking around you. Notice the individuals seated inside the restaurants you pass by. Dive into topics you have no prior knowledge in. Cook a new dish for dinner. Try a new form of movement. Take a road trip. *Simply continue to invest in expanding yourself.*

What these minor experiences demonstrate is that small shifts can make a difference. Through these actions, where you are aware, grounded, observant, and receptive, you will see that this too shall pass, because when you move through life, so does the energy in and around you.

WHAT IF WHAT YOU'RE
EXPERIENCING RIGHT
NOW IS PREPARING
YOU FOR WHERE
YOU'RE HEADED NEXT?

When life feels stagnant and when progress feels elusive, resist dismissing it as a wasted period. Instead, see it as a sacred pause orchestrated by a Divine hand, offering you the invaluable trifecta of time, space, and energy. This is not a stagnant interlude but a deliberate layover, where God provides the grace to heal and release what hinders your next journey. Picture it as a cosmic workshop refining you for the grandeur that awaits, an opportunity to shed burdens and embark unencumbered on the next phase of your voyage.

In this contemplative moment, consider the baggage you carry—do you want to drag it as a heavy burden or step forward unburdened, free, and clear, ready to soar on the path ahead? This is a Divine amnesty for the weary traveler, an invitation to embrace stillness as the fertile ground where resilience takes root and transformation unfolds its delicate petals.

Romanticize Your Present Life

When your dreams come true—whether it be landing your ideal job, securing financial freedom, buying your desired home, finding your soulmate, connecting with a new group of friends, discovering your purpose, obtaining radiant health, finally affording the material possessions you seek—I am sure that you will feel happy. Once these manifest into your reality, it is inherent that you will feel joy any time you commute to your job, swipe your credit card, walk into your home, kiss your partner, laugh with your friends, fulfill your life's path, live with vitality, and wear the wardrobe you've invested in.

But you can also feel joy until those moments arise. You can still wake up and feel excited towards the actions you're taking to secure a new job, as it's giving you space to discover what truly will fulfill you. You can still feel proud for the ways you're choosing to save your money, knowing it'll reward you in the end. You can still feel enthusiastic when browsing through potential places of residence, even if none of them check off all of your wants. You can still feel passionate when conversing with new souls, although their role in your life may be brief. You can still feel thrilled when you try new activities and hobbies, even if you haven't mastered them. You can still honor your body for all that it does for you, even if it's not functioning exactly how you know it can. You can still add items to your shopping cart, knowing one day you'll be able to press the 'order now' button.

Don't reserve joy for when you finally have all that you wish for. It is meant to be felt in the now, to be experienced throughout the journey of arriving to where you are destined to be. Because the reality is, if you don't love the process of getting to where you're headed, you'll arrive at a place with a sense of emptiness. You thought that once you had everything you prayed for, all will be well. And then you will have it all, but it'll hit you—the 'all' that you will have doesn't feel like how you thought it would. You'll still have worries, challenges, and problems, proving that it was never about the job, prosperity, home, soulmate, friendships, purpose, health, or financial freedom. It was always about feeling joy and experiencing peace from within.

It'll dawn on you, once it's too late, that the joy and peace you sought is not made once you have everything; it's felt the deepest during your pursuit. And a sense of frustration will wash over you—the regret of not appreciating life when you had the chance. *Do everything you can to never have to live with that regret.*

Love Song

Even during my darkest days, I refused to surrender to despair. With every ounce of strength, I dragged myself outside, seeking solace in the ever-changing landscape of nature that resembled transformation. Amidst the hustle and bustle at the grocery store, I reminded myself that each soul navigating the aisles experienced their own burdens, yet they persisted, and so could I.

Alone in my car, drowning out the noise of my thoughts with the blaring melodies of music, I hung onto every lyric, praying for the artist to articulate the turmoil within me in a way that I was unable to. During my daily commute to my job, I buried myself in the pages of a book to seek refuge from the sterile glow of screens and immersed myself in worlds far removed from my own.

Slowly and unnoticeably, the darkness began to recede. For what were once categorized as "bad days" now shimmered with a kaleidoscope of beauty. Each moment held the potential for inspiration, grounding, or connection. Every sunrise brought with it awe, wonder, or bittersweet confusion. I danced between ecstasy and agony, embracing the full spectrum of human experience.

What, then, defines a day as "bad"? Was it the derailment of plans, the onslaught of obstacles, the weight of unshed tears? And conversely, what makes a day "good"? Was it the warmth of love, the spark of inspiration, the thread of connection woven between souls, or the thrill of encountering something new?

In this revelation, a seismic shift occurred within me. Suddenly, the lines blurred, distinctions faded. Hurdles became opportunities for growth, deviations from plans invited adventure, and heavy emotions were gateways to the deepest wellsprings of love and connection.

Perhaps, all along, my days had been bathed in goodness. It was only the whispers of doubt, the shadows of negativity cast by my own mind, that had obscured this truth. In embracing the fullness of each moment, in surrendering to the ebb and flow of life's tide, I discovered that every day held the potential for beauty, if only I dared to see it.

She was a lover at heart.

I poured my heart into tales of love, as if intimately acquainted, yet truth be told, the love I wrote about had eluded my grasp. In a vulnerable moment, confiding in a friend about my solo journey through my entire life, devoid of a hand to hold or a lasting love, I asked about the enigma of loving and being loved. *"I'm clueless,"* I confessed. *"I wouldn't know what to do, you know. How to love, what's too much and what's too little and what's just enough. I fear that I won't know how to truly love a man or navigate a long-term partnership."*

Her eyes widened in disbelief. She shared her confusion, marveling at the depths of my self-doubt and the belief that such deep feelings were beyond my grasp. In her eyes, the bewilderment echoed, questioning how I could perceive myself as incapable of experiencing the inherent depths of companionship. *"Love is all the same,"* she stated. *"You are a great friend, you have a pure heart, you have so much love within you. Whether it's toward your parents, yourself, your friends, your community, or a future romantic partner, you already know how to love!"*

In that instant, a revelation unfolded: I was created on the foundation of love, therefore it is inherent within me. It comes in all shapes and sizes, all forms and dimensions, but the essence of love lies in meaningful connection, empathy, and selflessness, encompassing a commitment to the well-being of others, acceptance of imperfections, and a deep sense of joy and fulfillment derived from genuine human connections.

For all my life, I was a master of facilitating and maintaining this. And the proof was right in front of me—healthy relationships with my family members, lasting friendships from childhood, meaningful connections fostered in adulthood, purposeful relationships with colleagues, and intimate bonds with my online community. Realizing the innate, powerful force of love coursing through my very core, I awakened to the truth that every action, spoken word, piece of art crafted, expression conveyed, and embrace shared, bore witness to the undeniable manifestation of the boundless love that is inherent to my existence.

I never questioned my capacity to love ever again.

WHAT MAY FEEL LIKE
ANOTHER MOUNTAIN
IN THE DISTANCE WILL
SOON BE SEEN AS A
MERE STEPPING STONE.

You are your own guardian angel.

One day you will find comfort in all of the moments you thought you'd never get through. The experiences that felt like the weight of the world was being carried on your back, those events that made you question your faith and very existence, the brokenness of your heart that led you to believe it will forever be closed off, or the confusion and desperation and shame that made you look at yourself in the mirror in full terror, not knowing the person you see in the reflection.

One day, you will come to understand that those seasons of life were not given to you as a punishment, but instead, were opportunities to show yourself the resilience, grit, and strength that you innately held. To be able to wake up each day, with a broken heart and a weaker mind, yet still have an ounce of hope that, *"Maybe today it'll get better or maybe tomorrow will be different or maybe a week from now my life can change,"* was your way of building your own courage, bravery, and faith. Even if you didn't know it then.

One day, a future version of yourself will look back on those moments, not with anger or resentment but with love and gratitude, connecting the dots in how every shift was giving you the opportunity to bloom beautifully, transform gently, and heal softly. You will come to understand that the discomfort was necessary in order to evolve, the drawbacks were essential in obtaining clarity, and the stagnancy was vital in realizing what truly matters in your life.

Because the truth is—you survived, and always will. All of it. What was once seen as impossible, is now your victory. What may feel like another mountain in the distance, will soon be seen as a mere stepping stone. If you find yourself struggling once again, remind yourself of this: someday, somewhere, there is a version of you who has survived this, looking back with compassion, peace, and appreciation in their heart for your current commitment to continue pushing through your journey despite the adversity.

Acknowledge the fact that you persevered each time, proving that you are your own guardian angel in this lifetime. You must use this knowledge as evidence—these seasons are not your breaking points but the phases of your becoming.

The Composer

Do not forget to allow yourself to feel joy when you are in the midst of a healing journey. You were born to feel alive, experience bliss, laugh fully, smile widely, feel inspired, explore far, play fearlessly, dance aimlessly, sing vibrantly, express love, and receive love. This life wasn't meant to be a battleground—there will always be experiences that test your constraints, but they can always be orbited with love. Love for yourself, others, and life. Never forget that healing is becoming whole, and the only way to become whole is to allow your heart to play every string that it was designed to.

Give yourself what you effortlessly give to others.

Give yourself grace when your heart is broken; that is how love gets in and how love gets out. Give yourself honor when your mind is perplexed; that is when negative thoughts are dissected and when positive thoughts are alchemized. Give yourself compassion as you transform; that is how you celebrate your triumphs and how you prepare for upcoming victories. In mirroring the kindness you give to others, your flaws become strengths in unconditional colors.

Dimensions

Some days you will need to do whatever you can to simply get by. Other days you will ride a powerful wave of inspiration, immersing yourself deeply in your passion projects. Some days your body will demand an unapologetic pause, begging for a sacred time of rest. Other days you'll feel an invigorating energy surge, pushing the boundaries of what you thought was possible. Some days you will find yourself in a trance, staring blankly at your wall with a sense of numbness as the hours pass. Other days, you will be the pure embodiment of effortless joy, dancing in your apartment at 10am with vitality pulsing through your veins. Some days, the idea of socializing will light up your spirit, leading you to make plans with every friend. Other days, the quiet embrace of solitude will call you, freeing you from any external distractions and noise.

I want you to understand that this is all normal. That this is what it means to be a human. Your entire essence is continuously adapting and mutating—who you were a year ago is not who you are today, and who you are today will not fully encapsulate who you'll become tomorrow. Knowing you are an ever-changing, transformative force, evolving with every dawn and dusk, you must not compare the energy of the various versions of yourself with one another. It's not about always operating at full capacity or setting unrealistic expectations of perpetual greatness. All you must aim to do is feel proud of the efforts you are putting in at each present moment, for those efforts are the only things within your realm you can control.

In moments of confusion, with conflicting signals from your body and mind on the level of exertion you have capacity for, simply place your hand on your heart, ask what it needs, and listen to its silent wisdom. I promise therein lies the answer. You may hear that your body genuinely requires rest, or that perhaps you are slacking, or maybe you do have the capacity to socialize. In this journey of self-discovery and growth, trust in the wisdom of your own rhythm, for it is in the harmony of your highs and lows that your true strength and potential shine brightest.

Submission

I used to beg the Universe for a sign that I was on the right path. Then it hit me—I don't need confirmation. This is my path and whatever happens is right. If it wasn't, I'd either be somewhere else or guided towards a new direction.

Playing Field

Do not judge yourself for fumbling as you learn something new; you've never done this before. Do not criticize yourself if results haven't been reaped yet; it's through repetition that you'll eventually get rewarded. Do not question yourself for wanting to try something out of the ordinary; taking action despite the fear is what fosters bravery.

How can mastery be expected where experience is yet blooming? Trust in your capacity to flourish amidst new levels, for every attempt, whether perfect or imperfect, is a testament to your relentless spirit of exploration and resilience.

For all the truth that you made me see.

My father's wisdom echoed in the back of my mind every single day. *"Life is beautiful,"* he'd exclaim, when experiencing the high heights of joy. *"Life is beautiful,"* he'd whisper, even when tragedies were taking place. *"Life is beautiful,"* he'd promise, as I'd be crying in his arms asking whether my health would ever get better. *"Life is beautiful,"* he'd reiterate, when my brother met the love of his life. *"Life is beautiful,"* he'd voice, when he was in the midst of financial burdens. *"Life is beautiful,"* he'd exclaim, while crossing off his travel bucket list. *"Life is beautiful,"* he would reflect, gazing at a photograph of his parents who never witnessed his life beyond his 28th birthday. *"Life is beautiful,"* he comforted, as we laid my grandmother to rest.

My father's resilience and capacity to see life's inherent beauty in every situation was nothing short of remarkable. His perspective was not just a passive acceptance but an active celebration of life in all its complexity. Whether he was encountering joy, facing hardship, or reflecting on his past, his consistent message was a beacon of light. To every soul he encountered, he imparted a sense of awe and wonder about the gift of life. His conviction was not just belief; it was a living, breathing testament to hope, touching lives and kindling a flame of faith in the hearts of those he met.

In acknowledging life's difficulties, I also embrace my father's wisdom. Life's journey is fraught with uncertainties and internal battles. I've experienced the mornings filled with doubt, the days clouded with fear about what lies ahead and within, the weeks filled with shame, the years with slow progress. But in these moments, I remember his words, a guiding light through the darkness. His voice echoes, a reminder that even in struggle, there is a beauty to be found and life to be cherished.

I extend this message to you with the same conviction my father shared: *Life is beautiful!* This phrase, simple yet accurate, is more than a mantra; it's a truth to be deeply rooted in your consciousness. Despite the challenges, the uncertainties, and the fears, both external and internal, I compel you to always remember this wisdom. Life, in all its complexity, is a beautiful and remarkable gift. Embrace it, live it, and let this understanding transform your perspective, as it did for my father, for me, and every soul he's echoed it to.

You're returning home, back to the lightness from which you were born. But what if the darkness holds the key to illumination?

In the depths of the shadows, where darkness wraps around you like an old, familiar cloak, I promise you this: there is a brilliance waiting at the end of the tunnel, a promise of light that transcends what you're currently experiencing.

As you step forward, each footstep echoes with the weight of uncertainty. You tread through the unknown, every step cautious, every movement filled with the burden of not knowing when this journey will find its conclusion. Yet, in the midst of this obscurity, you notice a glimmer—a flicker that defies the pervasive blackness.

It may reveal itself just a few feet away, be hidden behind miles of uncertainty, or be the light within yourself that has finally sparked, but there will come a moment when you catch sight of that ethereal glow. At first, you'll question its authenticity, wondering if it's a mirage in the vast desert of despair. Simultaneously, a realization will dawn upon you—a realization that, just maybe, this is the fulfillment of a whispered prayer, the manifestation of the hope you've been longing for.

This light, though feeble and distant, may not cast away the entirety of the shadows, but it serves as a beacon, a testament to the possibility of improvement, resolution, and a brighter tomorrow.

Why, you might ask? Because there must be. We understand, deep within us, that nothing is absolute, that all things are transient, and this experience will one day be a thing of the past. As you approach the culmination of this arduous journey, you will look back and acknowledge the truth: you not only traversed the abyss, but also realized that it was through that darkness that you emerged into the embrace of the light.

It has been right in front of us, all along.

In the intricate reality of human existence, our truths are laid bare through nature's poetic choreography. Like the moon, we rise and fall, traversing myriad phases, ever-changing, ever-evolving. Similar to the sun, our essence radiates through space and time, vibrant colors painting an untold story, our presence resilient, not tethered to mere visibility. We, like clouds, are a fusion of diverse particles, each unique in shape and size, our very existence a masterpiece of individuality.

Mirroring the trees, we embody transformation, defying the constraints of a set timetable, resiliently shedding and rebuilding through every season, standing tall even during a loud storm. As caterpillars morph into butterflies in the silent cocoon, we, too, undertake a journey from struggle and limitation to the freedom and beauty of a new beginning. In the embrace of passion, like fire, we find both creation and warmth, burning away impurities through unbridled destruction.

When we cease to perceive ourselves in isolation from nature's grand design, we awaken to the realization that every facet of our being mirrors the intricate workings of the world around us. Our transformations, stagnations, metamorphoses, and destruction are elements intricately linked in Divine creation. Embracing this connection, we redefine ourselves not merely as human beings but as forces of nature, integral to the collective evolution that pulsates through the very heart of existence.

THERE IS BOTH A
WORK-IN-PROGRESS
AND A MASTERPIECE
THAT COEXISTS
WITHIN US, AND
BOTH WARRANT
UNCONDITIONAL LOVE

Coexist

In every season of self-discovery, we embark on a quest to delve deep into our innermost shadows, committed to dismantling the barriers that confine us. It's a transformative process, where we recycle the negative energies into something of great value, ultimately resurrecting our true essence. With a spirit of curiosity and undeniable bravery, we confront our subconscious beliefs and thoughts, recognizing that therein lies the true obstacles we must overcome in order to achieve lasting inner peace. But remember, in the heart of this metamorphosis, as you courageously face the fire within, it's essential that you also celebrate and illuminate the inherent light that already resides in you.

You can embrace self-love while pursuing self-improvement. You can cherish your body while guiding it towards better health. You can feel inherently worthy, even as you navigate and establish your boundaries. You can trust your inner voice, even as you seek new wisdom and perspectives. You can find fulfillment in your present self while envisioning and working towards your future self. You can be proud of who you are while remaining open to growth and change.

Never underestimate the importance of honoring the aspects of yourself that you've come to cherish and nurture over the years. This version of you was not always born from ease, therefore we must honor and celebrate not only our magnificence but also the depths and lengths we went through to arrive here. This journey will consistently require us to transform, but embracing the full spectrum of our being is honoring the veracity of being a human: that there is both a work-in-progress and a masterpiece that coexists within us, and both warrant unconditional love.

Events do not have emotions tied to them.

The turmoil coursing through you doesn't emanate from the mere unfolding of events, for events are emotionless entities. Devoid of sentiment, they exist as transient passages that create the sum of our lives.

Instead, the source of your distress is found in your response to these occurrences. It's your mind forcefully proclaiming, *"This isn't how it should be,"* or grappling with the daunting question of, *"How will I conquer this?"* It's a resistance to the present, a rejection of reality unfolding contrary to your envisioned narrative.

Frequently, the stresses that entangle us are echoes of past patterns. The familiar dance between experiences and responses will continue until we understand the lesson embedded within. Until a new adaptive response is learned, we find ourselves ensnared in the same web of stress, repeatedly.

Consider the frustration of being trapped in traffic before a crucial appointment. Your gaze shifts anxiously between the clock and the congested road, heart pounding as your body prepares for battle. But the stress isn't birthed from the traffic jam itself; it arises from the stark contrast between the open road you envisioned and the gridlock reality presents.

Reflect on a romantic connection, where uncertainty clouds the once-clear skies. Moments of intimacy and shared bonds now obscured by a sudden shift in their energy. Your mind races, questioning your role, frantically attempting to mend what feels broken. Yet, the stress isn't born from the shift; it emerges from the shattered illusion that relationships are perpetually adorned in rainbows and butterflies.

In matters of health, despite your unwavering commitment to well-being, illness wraps its arms around you. The frustration intensifies as symptoms resurface, new challenges emerge, and you desperately try to pinpoint the moment everything unraveled. Yet, the stress isn't birthed from physical sensations; it evolves from the belief that you shouldn't be in this place or that perpetual tensions shadow you. It's the exasperation stemming not from the ailment itself, but from the gaping disparity between reality and the hopeful vision you had.

Perhaps these stressful incidents serve as signals demanding internal change. In their twisted manifestation, they offer a chance to revisit unresolved patterns, urging us to delve deeper into our suffering, to comprehend its root, and ultimately rewrite our narrative. In order to create space for our desires, facets of ourselves that do not align with that version of us must undergo a symbolic death. Could it be that the very purpose of stress is to illuminate the parts of us—character, beliefs, reactions—that demand cleansing?

Embracing this perspective, you may find yourself once again ensnared in a traffic jam. Yet, your reaction is one of nonchalance, immune to the agitations over things beyond your control. A shift in a relationship's energy no longer casts a shadow of overwhelm or burden; instead, you hold steadfast in the belief that what is meant for you will always stay. Confronted with a resurgence of health challenges, you resist the familiar descent into overthinking. Instead, you interpret it as your body delivering a message you are finally prepared to receive, granting you the ability to obtain deeper freedom you've yearned for.

It's not that external events have undergone a dramatic metamorphosis; it's the transformation within you, in how you respond to them. Through this shift, you not only shatter the recurring pattern but also internalize the lesson. Your mind undergoes a purifying catharsis, leaving you prepared to wholeheartedly embark on the subsequent chapter of your existence.

Transitions

No matter how far we progress, setbacks will inevitably find us again. They're not just hiccups; they're emotional earthquakes that shake the very core of our being. Like ghosts from our past, they haunt our hearts with memories we thought we'd buried deep. They resurrect old wounds, reminding us that healing is never a linear path. The scars we thought had faded are suddenly reopened, raw and bleeding once more.

Setbacks don't discriminate; they appear from personal disappointments, unforeseen detours, or the cruel twist of fate. They come in myriad forms: a relapse of illness, shattered relationships, or the wreckage of our once-glorious plans. Each setback is a battle cry, a challenge to our resolve, a test of our resilience.

The harsh reality of setbacks is their uncanny timing, often striking just as we're on the brink of improvement. It's an annoying juncture where our initial reflex is to ask ourselves, *"Have I truly progressed, or merely buried the pain?"* We spiral into overthinking and self-doubt, not just about ourselves, but also about the purpose behind the obstacle and whether we can overcome it. Despite our efforts to maintain optimism and use this moment to strengthen our faith in a higher plan, we often regress to old habits—thoughts, behaviors, and beliefs we assumed we had transcended. This only compounds the frustration; now, it's not just the setback itself that infuriates us, but also our reaction to it and our struggle to change it.

However, amidst the chaos and despair, deep down we know that every setback is followed by a remarkable comeback. It's the yin and yang of life, the cosmic balance that ensures growth and blessings spring from adversity. It is the only cycle that tests our self-doubt while simultaneously strengthening our self-trust.

Knowing this to be true, we must embrace these obstacles, to meet them head-on with courage and grace. Perhaps a setback is a gentle nudge from the Universe, urging us to reclaim the power we've given away. Perhaps it is a signpost pointing us towards our true path, guiding us towards a destiny more aligned with our deepest desires. Or perhaps it's something even simpler than that—to give us a taste of the person we once were, in efforts to compel us to keep going.

You see, we frequently fail to recognize the strides we've taken. Rarely do we pause to acknowledge the milestones achieved, the beliefs reshaped, the thoughts released, and the patterns shattered.

Consider this: could the discomfort and unease in your current mode of operation be proof of your growth? If you find yourself grappling with frustration during a setback over your thoughts, actions, and behaviors, pleading, *"I don't want to be like this"* or *"I no longer want to act this way"* or *"This isn't the real me,"* could it not signify the shedding of aspects of your former self that no longer resonate with who you are becoming? If the familiar ways of the past no longer offer solace or ease, perhaps it's a sign of your transition to a new realm of existence. Perhaps it's the confirmation that you are indeed doing everything right.

So let us not shrink from setbacks but embrace them as the catalysts for change. They are proof of our progress thus far and affirm that we are ready for more evolution.

PERHAPS A SETBACK
IS A GENTLE NUDGE
FROM THE UNIVERSE,
URGING US TO
RECLAIM THE POWER
WE'VE GIVEN AWAY.

Can you embrace the present moment fully without the echoes of the past, allowing yourself to truly live in the now?

At times, we find ourselves searching for deeper meanings in situations, convinced that there must be some symbolism to decipher before we can proceed. Yet, in this pursuit, we often only succeed in driving ourselves to the brink of madness. We try to comprehend what is not yet meant to be understood, inadvertently obstructing life's natural course of revealing its purpose through the passage of time and the grace of patience. In our desperate attempt to control the narrative and engineer a specific outcome, we inadvertently stifle life's inherent wisdom.

But what if all that life asks of us is to simply accept, to find solace in solutions that align with what we can control, and to continue living in the present moment?

The irony lies in the fact that it is precisely when we relinquish our grip on understanding and surrender to the flow of existence that clarity and insight effortlessly find their way to us. It is in these moments of release that epiphanies dawn upon us, not because we tirelessly sought them out but because our minds were finally clear enough to perceive what was previously obscured.

Timeless Innocence

As I delicately turned the pages of dusty photo albums, read through old journals, and rewound grainy tapes from my childhood, a bittersweet symphony of nostalgia and grief enveloped me. I found myself entranced by a version of me that time had obscured—the little girl with an innocent, joyous smile, a soul filled with pure love, free from the complexities of life. Her laughter was a spontaneous melody, her love an unguarded oasis, free from the shadows of trauma or the distortions of fear. She existed in a realm of presence, glowing with a fearless radiance, always dreaming big and far.

Encountering these artifacts of a bygone era, I embarked on an introspective journey. Questions surfaced like ripples in still water: Where did that carefree child vanish? At what precise moment did the seamless transition to complexity occur? Have I evolved so deeply that this past self seems almost unrecognizable? Amidst the unstoppable flow of time, I wonder, can I find a way back to the simple joys and fearless spirit of my younger self?

As I revisited those tapes and delved deeper into the photographs and journals, a heartfelt realization dawned on me, piercing through what I had initially missed. Indeed, the journey through adulthood has sculpted me in myriad ways, yet, nestled deep within, my core essence, that unblemished purity of spirit, has remained untouched, steadfast through the tides of time and change.

In the various snapshots of my childhood, each photograph captures a younger me, her eyes sparkling with unspoken stories, her smile broad and unguarded. My laughter in every video echoed, pure and unrestrained, an uninhibited expression of a soul not yet touched by the weight of self-consciousness. My gaze swept across bustling rooms, imbued with an insatiable curiosity, a child's innate fascination with the wonders of the world. My expressions of love were generous and instinctive, manifested in spontaneous kisses and enveloping hugs, given freely to my friends and family. Each word I penned, even then, carried a weight beyond my years, a level of self-awareness that sought to explore and make sense of life's depth. In these memories, every moment and every gesture was a testament to a heart that perceived the world not just as it was but as it could be—endless in its possibilities and wonders.

Now, as I stand before the mirror as my present day self, the reflection reveals more than the passage of years. In it, I see the enduring spirit of my inner child, a reminder that amidst the evolution of my mind and the expanse of my experiences, the essence of who I am remains unchanged. My spirit, my soul, my limitless capacity for love—these are the unyielding pillars of my existence. They form the foundation of my being, unaltered and resolute. This recognition is not just a rediscovery but a powerful affirmation: the core of my being, radiant and steadfast, will forever illuminate my path through life. I am her, she is me, and together, we'll walk free.

PART 4

FREEING
THE SELF

Butterfly

No one ever warned me that freedom feels like grief—unveiling itself as a poignant farewell to the stories, identities, and former selves we've clung to. It's a paradoxical dance where the weight of shedding the past becomes the wings of liberation. In the tender embrace of this bittersweet metamorphosis, we find that freedom isn't an escape; it's the courageous homecoming to the authentic self.

Pray for a cleansing of the mind.

If you find yourself trapped in a mindset of scarcity or convinced that hard work alone is the key to manifestation, you may be living in the realm of survival. The pivotal initial step towards embracing abundance is the retooling of your mindset—an evolution from a state of lack to a state brimming with faith, trust, and abundance. Before your deepest desires manifest, you must first heal your mind.

This inner transformation sets the stage for the reception of all you aspire to receive—whether it be the financial prosperity you seek, the love you wish to draw into your life, the confidence you yearn to cultivate, the radiant health you yearn for, or the peace you hope to nurture. Because the truth is, your mindset is the epicenter from which everything emanates—it shapes every perception, every belief, every thought, every action, and every decision.

Therefore, God's deepest concern for you before he delivers his promises, is to first refurbish your mind, infusing it with clarity and ease. It is only in that state that you'll fully receive your desired blessings, and have the awareness to notice ones you may not have even asked for, but would've previously overlooked. For without a mind that is free, rational, clear, open, and calm, the things that emanate from it will be coming from the far end of the spectrum—attached, irrational, clouded, closed, and anxious. Think about it for a brief moment. Which end of the spectrum would allow your desires to manifest? Likely, the former.

It is worth mentioning, however, that the inner transformation doesn't always come easily. Be prepared to let go of everything you thought you knew. Be aware that your belief system will need to be altered. Be ready for experiences that test your constraints. Be willing to dissect every thought, every feeling, every reaction, and every emotion. Be conscious of the fact that in order for a new life to be created, a new you must emerge. Whatever door you intend to open towards the next phase of your life where your wishes will be granted, the prerequisite is a mind attuned to that same frequency.

The biggest indicator that you're ready for this cleansing is when your prayers shift. Rather than asking for specific desires, you ask for a new mindset. Because somewhere deep within you, you know that when that prayer is answered, so will everything else.

When the moment comes, do not resist it and instead, go right through it. This a loving act of restoration, a process that seeks to liberate you from limiting beliefs, fostering a mindset that not only believes in the abundance that awaits but also trusts in the Divine timing and benevolence. God's profound care for you is revealed through this meticulous restoration, aiming to fortify your inner world so that you may confidently stride into the fulfillment of the promises granted to you.

Forty Years

This is life. It's real, it's beautiful, and then it's confusing. It's wonderful, it's heavenly, and then it's challenging. But ultimately, it's the only one you have. So if you resent it, if you are unhappy with it, if you are yet to be fulfilled by it, you must not doubt your ability to change it.

To yearn for a different life isn't just a wish; it's a belief that tomorrow holds the promise of transformation. Perhaps in the tranquil space between the moon's descent and the sun's rising, your heart finds solace and your spirit soars.

We've Been Here Before

Your reality is a reflection of your consciousness—an intricate mirror that echoes your beliefs and perceptions about yourself. Each manifestation is a living expression of your inner world, shaped by the entirety of your subconscious mind. If you find yourself caught in cycles of unfavorable experiences, it's an invitation to dive deep into self-reflection. What have you yet to notice about yourself that perpetuates these manifestations?

This introspective journey becomes the catalyst for transmutation, triggering immediate shifts in your reality. Alter one aspect of your self-perception and your frequency undergoes a swift pivot. It's a quantum leap into a new state of consciousness, shedding beliefs and values that no longer align, liberating you from old patterns and behaviors.

Remember those moments when you set a boundary and witnessed an immediate shift in a relationship? It happened because you changed, and the relationship had to adapt or fall away. Perhaps you once held a subconscious belief that prosperity eluded you. The moment you recognized your worthiness, job opportunities flowed in effortlessly. Embrace the memory of embodying self-love and dispelling the belief of loneliness; didn't a parade of new connections follow, affirming your innate lovability?

In essence, you've danced with these perception transformations before, perhaps without fully realizing it. Now, recognize the incredible power that exists inside of you that can shape each category of your reality. You already have the forces needed to consciously evolve your self-perception.

Journal Entries

High above the Spanish terrain, I found myself immersed in the intimate pages of my past. Each word etched by the hand of a soul navigating her mid-twenties. As I read through the passages of time, my heart resonated with the echoes of my former self. A soul that bared its vulnerabilities in the ink-stained confessions of each journal entry. Health, a relentless companion in those pages, dominated the narrative of my struggles. Daily, I chronicled the pain, a silent plea for release, while always concluding each page with a fragile declaration, *"God, I still trust you."* Yet, in the quiet corners of my being, trust lingered like a flickering flame, never fully illuminating.

A wave of dissatisfaction surged within as I flipped through the chronicles of my own suffering, questioning the absence of jubilation in those journal pages. Why did I not commemorate the joy that played in the background of my life? Where were the accolades of success, the shared laughter, and the souls that left a permanent mark on my life? What about those moments when I fell shamelessly in love with the person staring back from the mirror and the life generously given to me? Why did I actively choose not to document the beauty in my life?

In this introspective flight, I discovered the unintended consequence of my therapeutic prose. My words, initially intended as a cathartic release, had morphed into shackles that bound me to the belief that I remained unwell. Each written expression was a daily confirmation and reinforcement of the unhealed wounds I carried within.

In the air above Spain, my self-awareness led me to make a vow with myself. A promise to break free from the habitual practice of documenting pain and instead, embrace the kaleidoscope of life's brilliance. The ink that was once a conduit for despair transformed into a beacon of light. From that moment forth, my journals held the rhapsody of my existence, chronicling the trials but mostly the triumphs, the laughter, and the unwavering growth that danced in harmony with my evolving spirit.

By not reinforcing a certain belief and instead, documenting favorable ones, I allowed my state of being to gradually be altered. It was as though the less energy I gave towards that one aspect of my life, the more energy I had towards all of the other ones. And that was when my life truly began to change.

Table for Four

There have been junctures in my journey when life was filled with vitality, toxic whispers muted into silence, joy emanated brilliantly, and my smile stretched wide. Yet, inevitably, a catalyst would emerge—whether a trigger, a health setback, or a disproportionate focus on life's imperfections rather than its harmonious tapestry.

In those pivotal moments, I found myself caught in an ancient cycle: retreating to the confines of my apartment, embracing prolonged solitude, and investing excessive time in the pursuit of healing. I erroneously believed that a return to greatness mandated perfection in every facet of my existence. I convinced myself that resuming the embrace of life required operating at an unwavering 100%. I grappled with granting myself the grace to tread upon this earth in all my messy, unresolved glory.

I was so deep in my head on healing that I forgot anything else could possibly exist. There were days cocooned in the comfort of home, shielded from the external world, where every spare moment was devoted to channeling energy into spiritual practices and mindful rituals. Initially driven by a genuine thirst for deeper understanding and a desire to unearth subconscious truths, I sought to liberate myself from the weight of suppressed emotions and the burden of an ailing body. These endeavors, born of pure intentions, evolved into the very foundation upon which I built my existence—a root anchoring my spirit and fostering my growth.

However, with time, what began as mindful routines metamorphosed into mindless obsessions. Hours once spent in reflective contemplation, somatic journeys, and deep breathwork multiplied unchecked. What had initially been a pathway to mindfulness gradually transformed into a hazardous obsession, as I perpetuated the belief that liberation required unearthing ever-deeper layers of subconscious thoughts. I unknowingly became entangled in the rush to expedite the healing journey by attempting to tackle everything simultaneously. *But that's not how it works.*

Caught in a loop of accepting my present reality while simultaneously yearning for a future unburdened, I grappled with the inherent contradiction. The coexistence of these truths proved impossible—I faced a stark choice between wholeheartedly embracing the present or pining for an unknown future. Despite my awareness, I persisted in self-imposed seclusion, trapped in a stagnant state, neither progressing nor regressing. What crucial element was I overlooking?

One morning, I fervently prayed to God, pleading for unmistakable guidance. *"Make it so obvious where I'm giving up my power. Let the realization strike me the very moment it happens. Show me the areas where I contract in spaces ready for expansion. Illuminate, with crystal clarity, the ways I operate that deviate from the alignment and integrity my evolving soul is ready to become."*

Several hours later, I found myself gathered at a dinner table with cherished friends. Amidst delicious food, shared laughter, and heartfelt advice, joy surged within me, rekindling a sense of vitality. I started to lose sight of the challenges that consumed my thoughts hours before, gradually becoming aware of the beauty that had long been overlooked and dismissed in my life. The transformative power of this simple change in the environment with kindred spirits got me thinking—why was I depriving myself of such enriching experiences, filled with genuine human connection?

With Divine clarity, the Creator responded during that dinner—I realized that the intense effort invested in healing, the self-imposed seclusion, and the waiting for radiant health were unnecessary prerequisites for fully embracing life. The Creator's message was unequivocal: I didn't need to strive for perfection. I simply needed to keep moving forward, placing myself in environments that fueled my soul and surrounding myself with beautiful people who inspired me. *All I needed to do was act as the version of myself I was so ready to become.*

While on my way home, I began contemplating about the person my soul was ready to transform into. The version of myself that I sought to embody didn't demand excessive hours in solitude or an overindulgence in spiritual practices. She wasn't fixated on perfection. Rather, she embodied balance—engaging in mindful practices at home while also partaking in the joys of the outer world, finding moments of solitude but also relishing the company of lovely souls. She prioritized her health without neglecting the joy of indulgence. She fully embraced the present for what it was while also envisioning the promising possibilities of the future for what it could be.

This experience reshaped my perspective on the ways we can heal ourselves. It unveiled the realization that powerful truths aren't exclusively unearthed in the stillness of spiritual practices. Instead, they can lie in plain sight— amidst new environments, in the company of others, and within simple conversations. Recognizing this, we must master the delicate art of balancing stillness and activity in our quest for liberation. The journey to freedom unfolds not just in moments of solitary reflection but also in the dynamic interplay of life's vibrant experiences.

YOU NEVER KNOW
WHEN YOU'LL MEET
SOMEONE WHO WILL
CHANGE THE COURSE
OF YOUR LIFE.

The Untethered Soul

I embarked on a quest to rediscover the latent strength within my body, to test its limits and unveil its deepest capacity for healing, transformation, and adaptive function. I was craving a visceral experience that transcended the confines of my mind—a physical pursuit aimed at immersing myself in the tangible sensations of strength, wisdom, and power dwelling within. The chosen avenue was Equestrian, though I stood at the threshold, unsure of where to begin or whether I was capable.

Ever since childhood, a magnetic pull towards horses had always captivated me. My grandfather enjoyed horse betting and I once volunteered at a barn in my teenage years, so perhaps that was the origin. The mere sight of these majestic creatures in a field evoked an instantaneous wave of calmness and peace, sensations that persisted into adulthood. Despite having ridden only once as a child, my fascination remained unexplained, except that these creatures embodied the very essence my soul longed for—angelic freedom.

In the mysterious way that the Universe orchestrates events, a friend I had met online, a connection nurtured through digital exchanges celebrating successes and sharing inspiration, finally materialized in the physical realm after three years. Our meeting, set against the backdrop of a warm summer afternoon over coffee, unfolded into an immediate and soulful bond, reinforcing my deep-rooted belief that you never know when you'll meet someone who will change the course of your life.

During our two-hour rendezvous, we chatted through topics such as our upbringings, differing healing journeys, passions, and the complexities of adulthood. But then, a seemingly serendipitous turn led us into a Divine dialogue, where my newfound friend shared her recent hobby of

Equestrianism. She described a therapeutic and healing sanctuary at a nearby barn, where weekly lessons became a source of solace for her. Astonishingly, she had never known about my desire to explore this activity, yet our meeting unfolded at the precise moment when the Universe seemingly conspired to deliver a deep message for me.

A few days later, caught in the crossroads of uncertainty about embracing a new passion or dismissing it as another fleeting interest, I found myself immersed in 'The Untethered Soul' by Michael A. Singer. This heartfelt book was a companion during my intense recovery from surgery, and was helping me reshape my very essence. In the quiet of my room that evening, I felt an intuitive urge to place the book down for a brief moment and instead, converse with God.

I resumed reading after stating a few prayers, only to discover an unmistakable sign urging me to embark on this uncharted journey. It was a moment of Divine synchronicity when, upon picking up the book, I noticed the cover I had fully overlooked—a captivating image of a horse galloping freely across the sand in front of an ocean. With laughter and gratitude, I looked upward and whispered, *"Thank you for guiding me."* The very next morning, I took the leap and booked my first session, propelled by a newfound certainty that this was a path I was meant to explore.

Weeks later, I was en route to that barn for my first riding lesson. The anticipation and giddiness that bubbled within me during the car ride resembled the joy of an inner child finally realizing a long-held wish. Recognizing the alignment of circumstances that connected me with my friend, the timing of our conversation, and the impending experience awaiting me, I sensed the hand of Divine orchestration once again.

Naïvely, I believed Equestrianism appeared deceptively simple from a distance   galloping, reins in hand, maintaining a straight posture. Little did I know the intricate dance that awaited me. The reality unfolded as I grappled with 50 simultaneous tasks, all demanding seamless execution while projecting an image of effortless grace. *Calves in, back straight, elbows slightly bent, hug the horse, look straight, move up and down, heels down, hands centered, engage the core, check the stirrups, and remember to breathe. Jesus Christ.*

As I navigated through the session, the complexity of riding revealed itself. Fifty tasks, seemingly contradictory yet harmoniously executed, engaged muscles previously untouched, required new breathing rhythms, and demanded balancing atop a creature inherently inclined to gallop freely. The effort to appear effortless was both challenging and humbling.

This brief yet intense experience illuminated my body's remarkable adaptability and capacity for learning. It demonstrated that, at any given moment, both body and mind can evolve, heal, and function in ways previously unexplored. Within the confines of that riding ring, my mind found freedom from external concerns, and for 30 minutes, it focused solely on the present task. My body adjusted to new parameters and learned how to leverage previously unused muscles, proving that my brain can establish novel neural pathways even within a short timespan.

Walking out of the barn and back to my car, a remarkable sense of excitement and gratitude enveloped me. Not only had my intention materialized in a beautiful way, but also my faith that everything unfolds exactly as it should, had also cemented further. In a delightful twist, Divine intervention fostered a blossoming adult friendship, allowing me to step into an environment my younger self had longed for.

This marked the planting of a seed—the inception of experiencing what I can only describe as angelic freedom.

Open Journal: October 11th, 2023

Every day it seems like something new pops up that further tests my patience, strength, and faith. It's as though every time I feel like I'm on the brink of full freedom, another sign is shown that there is more I need to dig into. I don't get it but maybe I'm not supposed to. I try to surrender and I do, but maybe it's not enough. Part of me feels frustrated, because how much more can I take? When will this all end? I thought I was almost done with all of this but here I am, still unwell. I don't know how else to move forward. Is it less that I must do or should I strive for more? My intuition feels clouded but I no longer want to stay under these clouds. The sun is shining in so many directions and that's where I want to focus my attention. But I also need to release, as I feel stuck, frustrated, confused, and lost. This morning I asked myself, "Where do I go?" and that's when God responded, "Come back to me."

Open Journal: October 14th, 2023

For a while I was thinking about how perhaps I haven't healed yet because I have fear over who I would be and what my spiritual practices would look like if I didn't have the need to dig deeper. But I've now learned, I will always have this part of myself, regardless of the status of my health. Because, for me, spirituality is about connection—connecting with God and myself—and these practices continuously allow me to hear His voice and my own intuitive voice. Due to the power of both voices and the impact they've made, I will never not create time and space to tap into them. My health was the catalyst, but my curiosity is what will sustain it.

Libra Eclipse

I came to terms with an essential prerequisite for entering the next chapter of my life. In order for me to truly heal physically, I confronted the harsh reality that I must detach from the part of myself that was burdened by a weak body and an even frailer mind. This aspect of my being was the architect of my internal balance, still feeding the physical suffering I was facing, therefore in order to experience deeper healing, I had to release that layer's grip on me. Otherwise, the relentless cycle of anguish would persist.

I knew the road ahead wouldn't be easy, therefore I recognized that guidance from a power larger than myself would need to assist me during each step. Realizing that this old version of myself, with its accompanying suffering, couldn't coexist with my healed self, I fervently prayed to God, *"Free myself from myself."* This prayer was an unrestricted acknowledgment, void of limitations or expectations, recognizing a subconscious force unknowingly fueling the very suffering I aimed to overcome. I came to terms with the fact that I must be reborn, that a new self must emerge. The conscious awareness that I needed to change in order for my life to change was bittersweet, concluding that I was deliberately begging for a storm of trials, day after day, in order to be liberated from the past.

As always, miraculous answers unfolded, illuminating inner wounds that I was unaware of, that I courageously began to reprogram. Through breathwork and somatic journeys, I shed layers, and then I rebuilt new ones. I let go of limiting beliefs, and filled the void with empowering convictions. But the path itself was strenuous and taxing, where everyday I'd be confronted with another challenge, where every moment was a mixture of survival and transformation. It was as though this aspect of myself kept pulling me ten steps backwards anytime I took one step forward.

In countless instances, the urge to give up gripped me fiercely. On my knees, I pleaded for the weight of this burden to be lifted. Gasping for air, panic attacks consumed me, each breath a seemingly insurmountable challenge. Confronted by the biggest fear of all—the unholy self—I uttered shocking words like, *"God, I don't think I can do this anymore,"* and *"If this is what the rest of my life looks like, I don't want to be around for it."* A voice that wasn't my intuition came to the surface—brutal demons within that I needed to desperately detach from.

Yet, I defied my own darkness. Again, and again, and again. I stumbled, but with unyielding resilience, I lifted myself up. I persisted in trust. I persisted in surrender. And then, as it unfailingly does, a glimmer of light emerged, gradually overshadowing the pervasive darkness. I ascended from the ashes, reborn like a phoenix. Those transformative weeks, marked by adversity and triumph, have etched indelible strength into my soul. Upon reflecting, I can affirm that I would relive that pain ten times more, knowing that it paved the way to my liberated state that I now cherish.

This is a truth of human existence—it is through suffering that we truly savor the taste of bliss. Without such trials, how could we ever grasp the essence of genuine serenity? Without such desperation, how could we ever find gratitude for the lightness we emerge from?

It is now clear to me that such experiences are not to be evaded or dismissed; rather, we must boldly embrace them with wide-open eyes, receptive hearts, and attentive ears. Within these crucibles, we unearth not only invaluable lessons and profound wisdom but also the untapped reservoirs of inner freedom and unwavering resilience. And these are the moments your life changes for the better.

THE BREATH IS NOT
JUST LIFE, IT IS THE
KEY TO UNLOCK A
LIFE UNBOUND.

Inhale, Exhale

As I settled into the rhythm of a breathwork class, the guide's words echoed like a challenge, *"You might be here because you haven't taken a real breath today. Or since last week. Or maybe since the beginning of the year."* Skepticism flickered within my logical mind—I breathe every day, both effortlessly and with intention. How could his statement hold any truth?

Yet, as I delved deeper, a question arose from within— when had I last drawn a truly transformative breath? A breath so profound it acted as a cathartic release for all that had been silently carried? A breath that dislodged the weight of accumulated trauma, stress, anger, frustration, and sorrow. A breath that expelled every suppressed emotion and set it free into the ether. A breath that whispered to every cell, *"You are safe here."* A breath that felt like an embrace from my inner child. A breath that embodied absolute surrender.

Our bodies keep score of every moment of unspoken affliction and every experience with potential trauma, marked by the breaths we hold back. It is only through the visceral act of release that we can rewrite the narratives imprinted into our neurons, reshaping the very

DNA of our beings. In the span of 60 minutes, it wasn't just stifled breath that found liberation, but a flood of repressed emotions from the depths of my subconscious. Fear, anger, pain, guilt, embarrassment, and shame, once cloaked in shadows, now spilled forth. Trauma, unrecognized and un-acknowledged, surfaced with clarity. Tears unshed, screams unvoiced, and tensions unrelieved were now unfettered, flowing from me with each deliberate inhale and exhale.

As the final minutes of the session waned, I emerged not just with a newfound appreciation for the act of breathing but with a seismic shift within. I was not the same person who walked into that room; I was reborn through breath, transformed by the elemental power of air coursing through me.

I then understood the potent truth—the breath is not just life, it is the key to unlock a life unbound. And with one last, expansive breath, I opened the door to endless possibilities, to a world where each breath is a declaration of freedom, a testament to the intrinsic resilience of the human mind, body, and spirit.

I'm fascinated for the time being.

To trust God doesn't mean you have to always understand. But it does imply that you believe that there are hands to be held, drinks to be enjoyed, laughs to be shared, places to be seen, emotions to be felt, smiles to be expressed, love to be received, food to be eaten, music to be heard, films to be watched, and birthdays to be celebrated. Perhaps in that trust, we find that even just imagining and hoping for a better life is enough for us to keep moving forward.

Handing Over The Reins

The quickest way to surrender is to thank God even when you are in the midst of turmoil. By expressing gratitude for learnings that have yet to be absorbed from your challenges, you are making a declaration: *"I do not understand at this moment, but someday I will. And I will thank you now, because I trust that you will soon bless me with more than I have even asked for."*

Custom-made

When envy creeps in, urging you to compare what others possess that you lack, it's time for a shift in perspective. The things within your orbit—whether it's a friend landing your dream job, a sibling finding their soulmate, family members with radiant health, individuals with strong social circles, or those around you basking in financial freedom—are not mere chance occurrences or a Divine taunt highlighting your deficiencies. Instead, consider this: if someone in such close proximity possesses what you yearn for, what if it's a subtle cosmic nudge? Perhaps it's the Universe whispering that you're closer to your desires than you dare to believe and that whatever you're seeking can also happen to you.

Embracing this mindset is like unlocking a door to abundance from the shackles of scarcity. As you stand beside a couple radiating romantic love, an inner voice whispers, *"I'm destined to experience this level of beautiful connection, too."* As you witness family members living freely in their healthy bodies, revelation takes root within you: *"I will also attain that level of vibrant well-being."* Your friend's tales of financial triumph become a spark, igniting the belief that, *"I too can achieve financial prosperity."* The joy resonating from a relative's job satisfaction becomes a beacon, illuminating the path to your own professional fulfillment, whispering, *"I can feel that fulfillment too."* The people around you who have healthy friendships and a fulfilling social circle, leads you to trust, *"I will find my people, too."*

In these moments, the shift is not just in perspective but in the very fabric of your aspirations, weaving a canvas of possibility and empowerment. It's the belief that being in close proximity to what you desire not only signals its imminent arrival but also assures that whatever materializes will be uniquely tailored to your life experience.

This underscores that everything you receive is intricately crafted for you, demonstrating a Divine and personalized touch in every aspect of your journey. And isn't that exhilarating? Believing that whatever blessing unfolds is custom-made exclusively for you?

You are never too much and you are always enough.

I kept praying to God, *"Allow me to see myself the way others see me."* Soon after I found myself being tested—I was placed in the middle of deep conversations where people would compliment me, thank me, congratulate me, and celebrate me. I'd accept and express gratitude, but my responses were always empty, not because I didn't feel thankful but because I couldn't believe it yet. And when you can't believe something to be true, your reactions are equal to that level of vacuity.

I knew there was merit in their expressions. Logically, I was confident in what they said because I too was amazed by all that I had accomplished and conquered at such a young age and the wise, kind woman I had become, all on my own. But when I'd be in solitude, the only words I could hear in my mind were, *"You are still not enough for yourself. You must do more, achieve more, heal more, and be more."*

The lack of inner acceptance frustrated me, which ironically became the catalyst for me placing myself deeper into a realm of stillness, so that my thoughts could grow silent and God could speak within and through me. His voice was loud, yet subtle. Vague, yet clear. *"Go back to the beginning."*

He planted a reminder of who I once was, the infant that was born into this Universe who inherently was enough, without having done anything, without achieving anything, without healing anything, without being anything. I finally got clarity—the enoughness I've been seeking my entire adult lifetime has been with me since the beginning. Never lost, only forgotten. Always there, but often dormant.

This level of awareness is when the game changed. I'd find myself having new conversations where I'd hear similar compliments, congratulations, gratitude, and celebrations. But the reception was different, because I was different—a testament to the shift I facilitated within my own subconscious beliefs. Rather than vaguely acknowledging their kindness through mediocre words, I expressed a heartfelt smile and a genuine hug that were manifestations of the appreciation, satisfaction, and warmth of my heart. These gestures became a declaration that I was, indeed, enough for myself as I was.

I finally saw myself the way others, and God, always saw me.

Unlimited

Genuine liberation unfurls in the moment when someone extends their admiration towards you with, *"I'm so proud of you!"* and instead of merely offering thanks, you boldly declare, *"I'm proud of myself, too."* It's an empowering resonance that pulsates within, a declaration of self-worth echoing louder than any external validation.

IT'S NOT THE
EVENT ITSELF THAT
DETERMINES OUR JOY,
BUT THE MINDSET WE
CHOOSE TO EMBRACE
IN THAT MOMENT.

**This is what happens when you
change your belief system.**

Eight months after the release of my debut book, it soared to #5 on the Amazon Bestsellers List. But instead of reveling in this remarkable achievement, I felt an unsettling emptiness. Despite reaching a milestone I once dreamed of, I found myself haunted by a relentless pursuit of perfection, convinced that only the pinnacle of success at #1 would warrant true pride and joy. At this point in time, I wasn't enough for myself as I was.

Yet, as I stood at this longed-for destination, the hollow ache of dissatisfaction only grew louder, echoing the extreme question: what truly brings me a sense of achievement? If I couldn't embrace this moment of accomplishment, would any future success ever satisfy my longing for fulfillment?

This moment of reckoning became a catalyst for necessary introspection. Amidst the quietude of solitude, I delved deep into the recesses of my subconscious, challenging and reshaping my limiting beliefs. Because if that moment couldn't bring me satisfaction, then what hope was there for any future achievement to fill the void? What purpose did it serve to pour my heart into creation, to leave an imprint on the world, if I couldn't find joy in celebrating my own efforts?

With unwavering determination, I sought to unravel the chains of limiting beliefs that led me to that reaction. And as I emerged from the shadows many months later, I revisited my Amazon ranking. Not having reached the lofty peak of #1, but humbly nestled at #81.

In that moment, as I observed the numerical testament to my efforts, a wave of emotion engulfed me. *"This is it,"* I whispered to myself, feeling a surge of empowerment coursing through my veins. The realization washed over me like a tidal wave—this number, this modest #81, was a testament to the impact I was creating and the lives touched by my words. *It provided more pride than being #5 ever did.*

This shift in perspective illuminated the truth: it's not the event itself that determines our joy but the mindset we choose to embrace in that moment. In that realization, I discovered the power to redefine my journey, to find solace in the impact I was making, regardless of where I stood in the rankings.

Gatekeeper

In times of distress, you must challenge your mind: *"Who profits off feeding these emotions and thoughts?"* Certainly, it isn't you. The spiral is a trap; it doesn't serve you, and deep within, you recognize this. Emotional discomfort is a sign of an internal imbalance, an itch that urges you to reconsider the way you process your life. Honor your feelings and inner dialogue for what they are, but refuse them the power to overstay and overwhelm. You are not your emotions and thoughts, nor are you the story you've affiliated them to. Rather, you are the guardian of your own peace.

We're Only Here Briefly

Resist granting power to things that compel you to travel far from joy. No person, job, situation, challenge, illness, or obstacle warrants sacrificing your fundamental human need for pleasure. Whenever you find yourself distant from this feeling, never doubt your ability to return to it. Just one small step of allowance, one gentle shift in direction, can guide you back. Joy is hidden in the simple things—play an upbeat song, go for a walk in nature, cook your favorite dish, call your friend, try a new hobby, explore a new part of town, dance in front of the mirror, create, watch, feel. Begin there, and gradually, moment by moment, experience by experience, the distractions will fade. You'll not only find your way back home but also discover a deeper, enduring joy that resonates within, guiding you towards what truly matters.

The Breach

There is a deep truth we all know, yet tend to overlook in each present moment. That almost everything we worry about, fear over, or stress on never even happens. By fixating on what might occur, we miss out on the beauty and potential of the present. Our energy, precious and powerful, is too often spent on mere possibilities, leaving us caught in a relentless cycle of 'what-ifs.' This leaves us feeling depleted, constantly living in a state of survival mode.

Yet, the truth is simpler and more liberating: our future worries are often just mirages of past experiences. Despite our tendency to overthink into solving a non-issue, the future unfolds independently of our anxieties. What truly matters is our readiness to face whatever comes, with the wisdom that experience, not worry, brings.

In hindsight, we often find humor and a bit of wisdom in our past concerns. The worst-case scenarios we imagined seldom materialize. Instead, life has a way of resolving itself, often turning out not just fine, but better than we anticipated. Challenges are met, fortunes turn in our favor, and lessons are learned.

Our free will is undeniable, a guiding force in how we choose to live each moment and respond to life's surprises. While we cannot dictate every outcome, we can steer our journey with intention and grace, trusting that the greater forces at play will align things in a way that's ultimately for our best. This realization invites us to embrace the present, to live fully and fearlessly, with the knowledge that we are always equipped to handle whatever the future holds.

IN ORDER TO PROTECT
YOUR PEACE, YOU NEED
TO CONSISTENTLY RE-
EVALUATE WHO BRINGS
VALUE INTO YOUR LIFE AND
WHO TAKES IT AWAY.

In order to protect your peace, you need to consistently reevaluate who brings value into your life and who takes it away.

When the moment came to celebrate the publication of my first book, there was an absence of congratulations from some of my closest friends. Their silence was noted, but not dwelled upon. Yet, amid this disappointment, past connections resurfaced as acquaintances from bygone days reached out to share in my joy. But it was the unwavering support of those who celebrated not just this milestone, but every step of my creative journey, that reaffirmed the bonds of genuine affection and loyalty. These are the souls I have come to prioritize in my life, for they have taught me that true love isn't measured by proximity or frequency of contact, but by the steadfastness of their presence in both moments of triumph and moments of vulnerability.

In the aftermath of my surgery, the silence from my closest friends cut deeper than any physical pain. I held onto the hope that maybe they were just busy, but as weeks passed without a word, the disappointment gnawed at me. Yet, in the midst of this confusion, unexpected rays of kindness pierced through the darkness. From the distant corners of my social circle came messages overflowing with genuine warmth and support, a balm to my wounded spirit. Still, it was the persistent presence of those who checked in on me day in and day out, holding my hand through the darkest moments of my healing journey even months later, that truly touched my soul and reminded me of where true love resides. Those are the people I have invested my time and energy in.

It is only in moments of profound pain and overwhelming joy when the true essence of those around us is illuminated with stark clarity. It is in these experiences that we discern who walks beside us out of genuine love and who merely lingers for the sake of convenience. Therefore, as we continue to expand and grow, we must periodically take an audit of which people truly support us, and which are only present in moments that serve them.

Picture yourself standing amidst your circle of loved ones, each of their hands interlocked with another, encircling you with a shield of solidarity and warmth. As you stand in the middle and begin to journey through life, charting new territories and embracing fresh beginnings, this circle remains steadfast, a beacon of unwavering support. They move with you, step for step, no matter the direction you choose to traverse. Their love is not tethered to conditions or convenience; it is a constant, unyielding force that propels you forward.

But then, as you venture towards uncharted territories, whether in the depths of despair or at the pinnacle of triumph, you find yourself alone in your forward momentum. The once supportive circle, now rigid and unmoving, becomes a suffocating cage stifling your growth. Your spirit yearns to soar, to explore new terrains, to heal and evolve, but the people that once moved with you are now binding you to a stagnant existence.

In this moment of realization, you find yourself torn between the familiarity of the past and the beckoning call of the unknown future. You are forced with the decision to either walk back to where they stand or to break free from their constraints and walk ahead alone. It is in these pivotal moments that we discover the true depth of our connections, and the painful truth that not all bonds are meant to weather the storms of change.

Yet, even amidst the heartache of this revelation, there is a glimmer of hope. For once you break the shield of familiarity, you're able to pave the way for your own freedom. That is when the emergence of new relationships, ones forged from mutual growth and unwavering support, come to the surface. And though the path ahead may be uncertain, you take solace in the knowledge that true companionship transcends the confines of a static circle, and that with each step forward, even if at first you are alone, you are moving closer to finding those whose love knows no bounds.

But as we navigate the labyrinth of adulthood, there's an unnoticed sense of grief that accompanies that transition. We yearn for the simplicity of bonds forged in the innocence of youth and the way in which we had them. Yet, as time goes on, we find ourselves clutching onto fading memories but starved for the creation of new ones. We hold onto the hope that those we care about will evolve alongside us, or at the very least, journey alongside us in the same direction.

Some of my most enduring connections trace back to my earliest toddling steps, while others blossomed in the dawn of adulthood at 18, or even later in my mid-twenties. Yet, intertwined with these treasures are the painful lessons of letting go. Some of my once most important friendships dimmed as their light failed to match the warmth I offered, while others were shackles holding me back from realizing my true potential.

Deep in introspection, I find myself grappling with a perplexing question: if I can navigate the ebb and flow of time while maintaining certain cherished friendships, am I truly the one at fault when some friends choose divergent paths? As I intentionally nurture and enrich my connections, watching them flourish alongside me, it's natural to wonder why certain people falter to keep pace. Shouldn't love encompass the acceptance of our evolution, encouraging each other to blossom into the fullest expressions of ourselves?

It then begs the question: why do some struggle to embrace the metamorphosis I've undergone since our first encounter? I've grown, transformed, and found solace in a life aligned with my truest self. Isn't love synonymous with embracing this evolution, cheering on each other's journey toward authenticity and fulfillment? As I stand at the crossroads of introspection, I'm reminded that genuine companionship transcends the static confines of who we once were, anchoring us in the boundless expanse of who we're meant to become.

Through this self-awareness, we must truly realize that our worth is non-negotiable. We must refuse to shrink ourselves to fit into spaces where we're not valued, for by doing so, we believe that our essence deserves to be celebrated and nurtured, not diminished, by the company we keep.

Leading With Love

Time and time again, I'd find myself pouring my heart towards those undeserving, it then aching with the weight of unreciprocated compassion. The agony of constant disrespect wore me down, questioning why my love was met with disdain. Was this a reflection of my weak boundaries or their obliviousness to the love I poured forth?

As maturity unfolded, I grasped the painful truth—not everyone had a heart like mine. Self-awareness and the ability to empathize with opposing perspectives elude many, transforming their pain into a dark, bitter energy. However, true maturity isn't a checklist of completeness; it's an unwavering commitment to always lead with love—a realization I had to confront, whilst also acknowledging that not everyone shares this commitment and that I might not always receive that love back.

Being genuinely mature—regardless of age—is the art of guiding and influencing others with boundless compassion, empathy, and an authentic concern for their well-being. It creates a haven of positive relationships and a nurturing environment to forge collective triumphs. It demands prioritizing understanding, kindness, and emotional connection, sometimes even initiating tough conversations, even when the world delivers its cruel blows. It urges us to pause before reacting, listen over speaking, and communicate over withholding.

In life, true maturity is the powerful and empowering anthem of always being guided by love. Envision a world where every soul matures in this symphony, where the harmonious notes of compassion and understanding paint a picture of deeper, more fruitful human connections. It's not just an ideal; it's the melody of a transformed world, where hearts resonate with the power of love, creating an orchestration that transcends the ordinary and elevates humanity to a higher, more harmonious plane.

I pray that we can all arrive here.

TRUE MATURITY IS
THE POWERFUL
AND EMPOWERING
ANTHEM OF
ALWAYS BEING
GUIDED BY LOVE.

Is it better to speak or to die?

When you find yourself in an emotional car crash, where you've lost control of the steering wheel and have found yourself on the side of the road, broken and in shambles at the hands of another driver, I prompt you to muster up the courage to finally speak your truth—not for them, not for your relationship, but purely for yourself.

Because if you don't, your heart and body will continuously give you unavoidable signals. Your physical being senses something is off, that emotionally and energetically, there is an imbalance within. Your mind may send other messages, but you must trust the physical sensations of your body as a sign to voice what is buried within the depths of your being. Because the heaviness in your chest, the slower digestion, the purge of acne, the sore throat, the sleepless nights, the lethargic energy, the redness in your eyes...these are not just bodily symptoms, but instead manifestations of a being who's living out of alignment. And until you handle it externally, the internal will continue to bear the repercussions.

You will repeatedly encounter the same situation until the lesson is learned, hasn't anyone told you that? You have much to say, with little room to say it. But the moment you seize that small window of opportunity, or instead, choose to create it, you immediately stop allowing the 'what-if's' or 'but maybe's' to haunt you. The moment you decide to speak is the moment you gain inner peace and recalibrate towards alignment. Even if time has passed, or it's been a year since you last saw the person who has your heart, it is never too late. As long as you wish to speak for yourself and do so, you have nothing to lose and everything to gain.

Because to speak means to be vulnerable. It means you've dived deep into emotional maturity. It means you value yourself more than the way the other person does. It means you're breaking a pattern of silence. It means you're willing to cut the cord. It means you're facilitating inner peace. It means you're choosing yourself.

The future always remains an immense mystery, yet the undeniable truth is that you possess the freedom to follow the urgent calls of your heart and body in the here and now. The Divine powers will handle the details that come after, and will do whatever it takes to bring you to where you ultimately belong. And regardless of what transpires after you voice your truth, you must always look to find gratitude for the relationship you were part of. Despite the pain, heartbreak, or confusion, you would never be the person you are today without meeting them, and that is a blessing.

So if you choose to speak, you must softly credit this individual for giving you the opportunity, capacity, and courage to do so. For once you break free from the habit of concealing your emotions, you become changed forever.

The truth is, we don't have that much time with the people we love.

As we age, harsh realities dawn on us—our parents live separate lives than ours, and the days we share in their physical company grow increasingly rare. The best friends with whom we once spent every afternoon embark on their unique paths, and making a plan requires substantial effort and advanced notice. Living under the same roof as a sibling becomes a distant memory, replaced by a longing for those moments when they were just a shout away.

As we mature, we begin to appreciate the rarity of deep, honest, and soulful friendships. These are the companions who lift us up, support us through thick and thin, and offer solace in challenging times. These individuals are indeed rare gems. As we approach life's quarter mark, many friendships fade, leaving behind only those who truly resonate with our being. But this refining of our circle becomes a blessing, revealing friends who bring out diverse facets of our personality, challenge us, and ignite inspiration. We learn the invaluable lesson of cherishing those loyal ones who see our worth more clearly than we do ourselves, guiding us to nurture a deeper bond with our most enduring friend—ourselves.

As we navigate through life, we come to understand that romantic love often strays far from its cinematic portrayals, where the exceptions are just that—exceptions, never the rule. The dating world teaches us the rare luck needed to forge a bond that harmoniously blends physical, mental, and emotional attraction. It's an even rarer miracle when two souls seamlessly integrate into each other's lives. Yet, with maturity, we realize that enduring love blossoms when two individuals meet at the perfect juncture, both ready to embrace and equally invest in love's give and take.

Amidst this journey, we encounter trials that test our belief in love itself. Moments of realization that people change, that wounded souls can inflict pain on others, and that unrequited love is all too real. We grapple with whether we should reflect back the energy being given, or whether we should always bring our best foot forward regardless of reciprocation. Yet through these experiences, we learn that everyone has their own struggles, that the scars of unhealed childhood traumas linger and that some souls are destined for a chapter in our story, not the entirety. We come to understand that people's actions towards us are more reflective of their own inner battles than of our worth or identity.

As our lives continue to unfold, the dynamics of family evolve with the passage of time. Siblings embark on the sacred journey of matrimony, cousins disperse to distant horizons, and our respected elders transcend into a realm beyond our mortal grasp. The once-vibrant holiday dinner tables now echo with the absence of familiar faces, and the exuberant laughter of children no longer vibrates through the air. Amidst this shifting picture, we find ourselves seated at the same table, surrounded by new souls who bring a mirage of unique stories and energies. The sprawling gatherings of the past transform into intimate affairs, with a guest list distilled to a cherished few. In these quieter moments, a poignant blend of nostalgia for what once was and excitement for what lies ahead envelops us. The table remains a constant, but the faces have changed, marking the impermanence of life's journey and the beauty of each fleeting chapter.

As we age even further, we are forced to face grief when a loved one passes away. The unbearable aching of the heart no longer is just a reality in someone else's life, but something we now too have to face. Whether it be a short life or a long one, the death of a loved one will force us to rethink the way we showed up in that relationship, and at what effort. Questions might arise such as, *"When was the last time I saw them?"* or *"Did they know how much they meant to me?"* Yet, with adulthood comes the irresistible realization that life is incredibly short, therefore we must change our ways to make time for one another. No longer will we allow the excuse of being busy prevent us from connecting, because we recognize that there is nothing worse than living with the regret of, *"I should've spent more time with them while I had the chance."* We gradually become aware that our greatest hope lies in arriving at a point where we can truthfully declare, *"I loved with all my heart, and in that profound love, I find serenity at this journey's end."*

And so in these moments of reflection, we find that love, in its truest form, is not just about grand gestures or storybook endings. It's about the quiet, steadfast and continual presence in each other's lives, the respect that grows from shared experiences, and the resilience to weather life's storms together. This understanding leads us to cherish not just the moments of joy and celebration with these individuals, but also the mundane, everyday experiences that deepen these relationships.

So please, before it's too late, express your love to those who matter most. Say those three words the moment you feel it. Share the whispers of your heart, even if it's sudden or the future is uncertain. Speak your truth, no matter how daunting. Communicate the imprint people have on you, even if it feels unnecessary to do so. Unite individuals, even in moments of frustration where the obligation to bring them together weighs heavily on your shoulders. Whoever you're thinking about at this very moment, reach out to them. Don't shy away from expressing your feelings, not out of fear of rejection or the need for reciprocity, but as an open-hearted tribute to those who have left a permanent mark on your life. Because the truth is, we don't have that much time with the people we love.

WE EMPOWER NOT BY
TETHERING SOMEONE TO
OUR EXPECTATIONS BUT
BY GRANTING THEM THE
FREEDOM TO EVOLVE
ON THEIR TERMS.

If only you could see yourself in my eyes.

For what it's worth, there's an untold beauty in the act of seeing someone else's potential. It's a touching journey to envision a version of someone that transcends their current existence—a version yet to be fully realized, the version of them that God intended them to be. To witness their latent capabilities, to imagine the depths of their character, the beauty in their actions, the vitality in their lifestyle, and the transformative evolution they can undergo is nothing short of extraordinary.

In this intricate dance of connection, we find ourselves weaving together a portrait of their higher self, a reflection of the person they could become. It's a twisted yet lovely process, a mosaic constructed from the fragments of their character, actions, habits, gestures, and mindset that we've had the privilege to witness. As we meticulously take inventory of our shared experiences, conversations, and interactions, we peer beyond the surface, recognizing them not just for what they are now but for the inherent greatness they've always possessed, if only they could see it too.

However, a crucial distinction arises between seeing someone's potential and enabling them to navigate their journey independently, and the peril of waiting for them to realize their potential while sacrificing our own happiness. It's a delicate balance that often leads us to pause our own lives, stunting our growth out of deep care and admiration for the person before us.

We become captivated by the vision of their untapped potential, believing that because we can perceive it, they must too. Consequently, we find ourselves in a relentless cycle of waiting, hoping, and yearning for their evolution. Yet, all too often, we discover that they aren't yet ready or simply do not have the desire to embark on the transformative journey we envisioned. Since our precious energy is too fixated on their expansion, we tend to hinder our own evolution into our higher selves.

In these moments, it becomes imperative to transcend the boundaries of our emotions, always striving to see the best in the other and inspiring them to tread the path of self-discovery. However, an equally significant lesson emerges—the wisdom to discern when it's time to release our grip, allowing them to walk their own journey independently.

It is in this release that true empowerment lies. As we navigate the complex terrain of relationships, we learn that fostering growth requires both encouragement and liberation. We empower not by tethering someone to our expectations but by granting them the freedom to evolve on their terms. In doing so, we not only honor their individual journey but also reclaim the space to nurture our own happiness and personal growth.

It is in this subtle equilibrium that the most empowering connections unfold, where two individuals, inspired by the best in each other, are free to embark on their respective paths of evolution. And if one day their paths converge once again, their dynamic and relationship will be different. All because they individually cultivated their wholeness from within themselves.

Guiding Light

Recognize the reality that transformation is a personal journey. And so while you can't directly change another, you can always inspire them through your own growth and resilience. Believe that each person's evolution unfolds on its unique timeline, a process beyond your control. Yet, in this realization lies your power: to become a living testament to the potential within us all. By embodying the change you wish to see, you become a beacon of possibility, demonstrating the heights one can reach. Shift your focus from the futile effort of changing others to being an example of self-evolution by showing them, through your own aligned life, that they too possess the strength to grow and transform. Let your life be a radiant example of what it means to evolve one's mind and destiny, to become the person you have always dreamed of. In doing so, you don't just illuminate a path; you become the path, guiding others towards their own higher selves.

Be not wise in your own eyes.

Divine timing suggests that events, situations, or occurrences happen in accordance with a higher plan or order. In essence, it implies that there is a perfect and predetermined timing for everything to unfold in our lives, guided by a cosmic force.

Imagine peering through the lens of the Creator, whose perspective transcends our limited understanding. He not only discerns the intricate threads of our path but beholds a panoramic view, a celestial vantage point encompassing the myriad components interwoven into our soul's design.

During moments of impatience, we often fixate on our own rhythm, oblivious to the synchronicity of others' timelines—people, places, and cosmic forces entwined in a dance of evolution that eludes our control. From this bird's-eye view, we glimpse a kaleidoscope of simultaneous occurrences, each intricately linked to our growth and destiny, much of which remains beyond our influence.

Consider the pursuit of love—a desire that tugs at your heart, yet the ideal partner seems elusive. What if the Creator, in his Divine craftsmanship, is still refining and preparing your soulmate, ensuring they match the depths of your yearning and what will truly fulfill your heart? It's not a dismissal of your timing but a testament to the unfolding perfection in the eyes of the Creator.

In the realm of career, despite your relentless efforts, financial fruition may linger. Could it be that the Creator is meticulously aligning details from diverse counterparts or waiting for others to fulfill their roles before prosperity cascades into your life?

And in the quest for radiant health, even with mindful care, challenges persist. Perhaps the Creator beckons you to explore uncharted territories, encounter souls, and share experiences that ripple through society with a profound impact of collective healing.

We tend to interpret our circumstances through our own narrow lens, forgetting that every action, destination, and experience has been intricately woven into the fabric of our evolving, connected journeys. Release the tether of self-reliance; acknowledge that, behind the scenes, the Creator orchestrates the fulfillment of abundant promises.

Consider this: God's timing is not a distant concept but an imminent reality. What if your pursuit actually aligns perfectly with the cosmic clock? If you embrace this belief, how would you seize the next 24 hours? Who would you become, what thoughts would you harbor, what burdens would you release, where would your footsteps lead, and what actions would you undertake? In the embrace of Divine timing, your essence aligns with the Universe's heartbeat, pulsating in harmony with the rhythm of creation.

Freedom of The Self

Once you experience freedom, the only struggle that then remains is to never succumb to the chains of enslavement again. It beckons a realm where nothing can shake you, in a place where the forces of resistance cannot take hold, and where your heart refuses to be sealed shut ever again. True freedom demands responsibility, devoid of alibis, devoid of self-pity, and devoid of reliance on others. It's a journey where you propel yourself forward, applaud your own victories, and embrace vulnerability without a trace of fear.

To be liberated is to stand bare at the precipice of a cliff, ready to leap into the unknown without the safety net of a parachute. It's the audacity to articulate your truth, even when there are no hands to catch you if you fall. It's strolling toward a firmly shut door, armed with the courage to swing it open, despite being oblivious to the mysteries concealed in the room beyond.

Freedom is the acceptance that you are the guardian of your destiny—a realization that genuine liberation unfurls only when you unfurl as your authentic self. It is a declaration to the Universe that you will forge ahead, unshackled and unburdened, painting the canvas of your fate with the vibrant hues of your unrestrained essence.

PART 5

BECOMING
THE SELF

From insight to action.

Transformation doesn't occur when you have a moment of revelation or receive some Divine enlightenment buried deep within your consciousness. It occurs when you take that newfound understanding and bravely step back out into the world. It's in the gritty, messy reality of life where true evolution unfolds.

If you let those insights gather dust—untouched and unapplied—then what have you really gained? The same old patterns persist, the experiences stagnate, and your actions remain unchanged. The truth is, the abyss of uncertainty will feel uncomfortable at first, as the natural inclination is to cling to the comfort of familiarity. It's a relentless tug-of-war between your rational mind and the whispers of your heart, each vying for dominance.

Yet, to truly learn something profound about yourself and then have courage to alter your behavior in alignment with that knowledge—oh, that's when the seismic shifts of transformation truly ignite. It's a journey of integration, where you fuse your newfound wisdom with the fabric of your existence, transcending into a higher state of being. This is where the magic happens, where you not only transform your inner self but also the very reality you inhabit.

THE HOME YOU
CONSTANTLY CRAVE
IS REALLY THE HOME
YOU CAN ONLY FIND
WITHIN YOURSELF.

Create a declaration of who you are in the
world—who you currently stand as and who
you intentionally desire to be. Read it every
day, and watch your entire life change.

To myself: Allow your choices to reflect your hopes and
your dreams, and not your fears or your worries. Do the
things that scare you but that are energetically and intuitively aligned so that you can continuously expand and
grow. Feel childlike wonder and curiosity every day, and
trust your intuition to guide every action. Hold the same
compassion, love, and gratitude for yourself as you hold
for everyone else in your life. Create and co-create in a way
that allows you to feel more connected to God, your soul,
and your community. Always keep your heart open and
remember that nothing is ever worth closing your heart
over. Be humble and remember that we are all one. Allow
yourself to receive love and remember that you deserve to
receive as much as you give. Impact everyone you come in
contact with through compassion and connection.

To God: Please invite me into deeper reverence in my body,
allowing it to feel safe, relaxed and confident, and nourishing it in a way that feels closer to you. Please allow me to
feel my heart and keep it open even when I feel scared or
triggered. Please allow me to choose myself even when
I'm not feeling chosen by others. Please show me deeper
mirrors of myself so that I can see where I'm expanded
and where I'm not yet free. Please open the doors that
need to be opened and close the doors that need to be
closed. Please bring me a romantic love so beautiful, that
we expand one another into more authentic versions
of ourselves and foster an intimacy of love that feels as
though you are pulsing through the moment. Please allow

me to have deep appreciation for the small things and allow me to be fully present in the mundane.

Write your own version and then get ready. Your entire mindset and life will begin to change.

You can't flee your own self.

The home you constantly crave is really the home you can only find within yourself. What your soul yearns for is a place of infinite love, unbounded happiness, consistent security, and harmonious resolution. Yet, we often place the weighty burden of this pursuit in the hands of others or in distant environments, enduring an endless wait for that perfect external haven or feelings of a grieving loss once we depart paths.

The reality, however, is that in every journey and every embrace, you remain tethered to yourself. Whether wrapped in the arms of a lover or traversing the globe with peers, your constant companion is actually just...*you*. Therefore, the source of that void is not external energies lacking connection with your spirit but rather the bond between your heart and mind.

To break free from this ceaseless cycle, you must reflect on moments when pure happiness and tranquility enveloped you. What relationship did your heart and mind have in those moments? How did they communicate with one another? How did they work together to facilitate harmony? How did they support the varying desires each had? You may not recall the specific place or time, but you may notice that you were wholly present in those instances where your heart and mind were aligned. *You were the only constant.*

When you find peace within yourself and establish an eternal home from within—you have everywhere to go. And wherever you do, you will always be home.

Terminal A

The allure of the travel process has always captivated me. There's a certain magic in the prelude to departure—the thrill of anticipation as I meticulously check my packing list, the reassurance of confirming my passport's presence in the front pocket. Walking up to the check-in kiosk is a source of immense joy, engaging in a mental game to estimate how many pounds over my baggage might be.

Strolling through the terminal becomes an experience of absorbing the multitude of faces, each representing a fleeting encounter in the vast expanse of humanity. *"I wonder if any of these faces will be in my future dreams and I won't even know it,"* I think to myself. The selection of my airport look is a source of inspiration, a quest to perfect a balance of comfort, classic style, and practicality. I feel curious about those I see, contemplating the stories of strangers—what journeys they embark on, the reasons behind their travels, whether it's their first time on a plane together, or the unique dynamics of the family across the corridor. Every fleeting interaction becomes a source for wonder and imagination.

Surprisingly, I find joy in navigating the realms of security and customs. The repetitive chorus of TSA agents, bellowing the same instructions with unwavering passion—*"Laptops out, shoes in the bin, belts off"*—strangely comforts me. Perhaps it's the consistency in their voices that resonates, a shared dedication that I can't help but admire. The notion of being in a confined space, genuinely secure, surrounded by a multitude of strangers, each leading their own peculiar lives for diverse reasons, intrigues me. Getting a stamp from a new destination is a declaration that I, indeed, was here and there. We coexist in this transient moment, transitioning from one place to another, saying hellos or goodbyes, concluding one chapter or embarking on a new one, a collective yet individual journey.

I consistently opt for the window seat, a deliberate choice to immerse myself in the vastness below, an intentional act to feel small against the grand terrain unfolding beneath me. In that elevated spot, my thoughts find serenity, hushed into a tranquil rhythm. There's a unique peacefulness in the airborne solitude—no destination demanding my presence, no tasks clamoring for attention, no faces to meet, no conversations to engage. I am simultaneously unreachable and unapproachable, yet paradoxically boundless. Amidst the clouds, I find a sanctuary where I can read, write, watch, think, and observe, embracing the rare gift of physical stillness.

Yet, what is it about this aerial experience that consistently propels me to book another flight? It's not just the allure of the destinations that draws me in, but rather the captivating process of getting there that truly invigorates me. It's the anticipation, the ascent, the suspended moments in the sky that breathe life into my soul. Perhaps it's not the cities themselves that beckon me but the experiences woven into the journey towards them—the in-between moments that unveil a kaleidoscope of untold stories and uncharted emotions.

It's unmistakable that energy isn't confined within us; it permeates everything around us. From the moment we step out of our homes, navigate through an airport, and arrive at a new destination, we become conduits for the collective energy enveloping us—a force that holds the potential for remarkable transformation. The experiences we download and the memories we forge in these spaces linger, imprinting themselves not only in our immediate recollections but also elevating us to new heights for the foreseeable future.

The impact extends beyond the positive energy we absorb; it's also about sensing the void left behind in the spaces we once occupied—our homes, routines, and familiar environments. The person I am before embarking on a flight undergoes a metamorphosis by the time I return home. The energy of my residence is left behind, carrying only what resonates and is essential. In the emptiness, I infuse the vibrancy that novel destinations bring, filling the gaps and spaces with the richness of diverse experiences. Returning home, I step through the door as a renewed version of myself.

So, what is it that draws me to travel? It's the euphoric high—the intoxicating blend of anticipation, possibility, and the inherent energy that comes with the transient nature of these spaces. Each journey through an airport becomes a gateway to an elevated state, a portal towards a new dimension, and a fusion of emotions and energies that leaves an indelible imprint on the traveler's soul.

FOLLOW THE WHISPERS
OF YOUR SOUL, NOT THE
IRRATIONAL DICTATIONS
OF YOUR MIND.

**Follow the whispers of your soul, not the
irrational dictations of your mind.**

In the space between your comfort zone and your dreams, your dormant strength eagerly awaits its recognition. It's tempting to linger in the familiarity of your current reality, to cling to the structures that brought you to this moment, yet true magic unfolds in the uncharted territories beyond comfort's grasp.

Amidst the safety of the known, a subtle fear arises—the fear of abandoning the familiar to leap into the vast unknown. Yet, when have great things ever sprouted from the soil of comfort?

The most enchanting connections materialize the moment you cast aside your comfort and engage in a conversation with a stranger, activating a reservoir of courage that echoes in future interactions. The most extraordinary opportunities materialize when you defy your egoic doubts and send that daring email, elevating your confidence to pursue subsequent possibilities. The most powerful experiences unfold when you shatter your fears and attend an event where you know no one, leaving an indelible mark on your ability to be bold in the face of the unfamiliar. The rich fulfillment you've tasted emerges from creating something that impacts others, reinforcing the belief that anything conceived in the recesses of your mind can come to life.

Your dreams, regardless of their magnitude, were intentionally planted in the soil of your soul. These aspirations are not whims but God's imprints, placed in your heart by a higher plan precisely at the time when you're meant to embrace them fully.

Doubts may linger about your capabilities, about the very validity of your dreams, prompting you to question whether this vision is mere wishful thinking or the destined path meant for you to tread. Yet, despite these fears, the magnetic force that should pull you is not the mere attainment of that dream, but the exhilarating journey of pursuing it. The thrill that accompanies the exploration of new facets of yourself as you stride towards manifesting that dream will render you awestruck and filled with wonder.

I assure you, amidst the moments of tireless work and relentless pursuit of greatness, you will surprise yourself. The discoveries made within you—talents yet unearthed, strengths waiting to be acknowledged, grit rising to the surface, and creativity unfurling—will leave you marveling. Every dimension of your being, intentionally crafted, is poised to achieve greatness, and the journey toward fulfilling your dream is the crucible that unveils these latent treasures within you.

I know this to be true because I've experienced it, time and time again. Amidst a work trip back to Atlanta for a shoot, I found myself grappling with uncertainty about my purpose there, as my role appeared vague and my efforts straightforward, leaving me to wonder why God had led me to this city once again. I silently conversed with God as I walked back from the studio to my hotel, thinking, *"I'm not sure why you brought me here, but I'm excited to find out."*

On the second day, during the same morning meditation I've been doing for two years, I found myself visualizing an untapped dream that had been silently shaping within me, one that I had failed to fully recognize until that very moment. Like a crystal-clear revelation, this dream emerged—to expand my writing beyond just books, but into films as well. Screenwriting was the said dream, and while far-fetched, it was beautifully aligned, weaving together my drive, interests, passions, talent, journey, and creativity into a cohesive vision. A skeptical voice echoed in my mind, asking, *"What makes you think you can achieve that?"* But I immediately dismissed it, understanding that God wouldn't have placed me in that environment, unveiled that realization, or planted that vision in my soul without a deeper purpose.

Hours later, fatigued yet determined, I reluctantly debated attending a client dinner, as it meant stepping beyond my comfort zone into the unknown, unsure of the attendees and plagued by self-doubt on whether I was capable of holding dialogue with individuals who were far more experienced than I was. But then I pondered the potential missed conversations, connections, and experiences if I chose not to attend, which I determined was a regret I wouldn't be able to live with. So, I decided to go.

Seated at that dinner table among unfamiliar faces, I found myself immersed in conversations about the very dream I had meditated on earlier. Yet, it wasn't my doing, the topic sprang from these souls who sat across from me. The individuals I engaged with were seasoned experts in the film industry that I was newly exploring, holding years of success and an intricate understanding of what I was eager to embark upon. They began to speak about their work, where I attentively listened, asked questions, and sought advice. I even publicly declared to them this new dream of mine, which was my way of cementing it as a confirmed destiny that I proudly embraced.

The enchantment of the entire experience lay in the simple act of nudging myself beyond my comfort zone and immersing myself into that unfamiliar terrain—an unintentional stride that brought me closer to what I aspired to achieve. Had I not taken that step, the envisioned dream might have felt less vibrant, my self-belief may have wavered, and the reservoir of knowledge I acquired would have been less rich.

When I returned home, the signs magnified. Random messages online led me to forge new connections with established writers in the film industry. One ordinary day during my usual walk to work, I stumbled upon a film set with cameras, equipment, and producers spanning the street. Soon after, an email from my building management confirmed a movie was to be filmed on my block. With intrigue and excitement, I soaked myself in the cinematic atmosphere by making it a habit to explore my neighborhood after work. To my amazement, critically-acclaimed screenwriters began engaging with my work online and sharing it with their audiences. Conversations with close friends entered a new direction as I shared my dream, prompting them to offer introductions within the industry. It's as though the moment this dream was planted in my heart, the Universe began to conspire in my favor to allow me to feel it, experience it, and ultimately, guide me to fulfill it.

Yet, what captivates me extends beyond merely reaching the envisioned success; rather, it's the exhilaration of continually pushing and challenging myself to scale greater heights. It's not just fulfilling a dream; it's about becoming the person who can fulfill it. To have a desire planted in your heart instills a Divine nudge that something bigger awaits, that a new journey has been set forth for you, that there is a new version of yourself yet to be met and that a new world can envelop you.

This, in essence, is the heartbeat of any dream—the desire to always strive for greatness and to live a life worth holding onto.

**Your only goal for each day is to
be open to what flows in.**

Life unfolds not according to our meticulously crafted plans but in the unpredictable dance of unforeseen moments. You can meticulously script your days, plan each activity, set your itinerary, and envision the scenes, characters, and locations of your life. Yet, as life inevitably does, it throws unexpected twists your way.

A friend's invitation interrupts your schedule, leading to a much-needed coffee catch-up. A prolonged phone call alters your priorities, steering you away from a timely email but providing the mental solace you didn't know you needed. A malfunctioning vacuum transforms a cleaning day into an online shopping venture, unexpectedly meeting a different need. A restless night shifts your focus from a planned workout to much-needed rest, aligning with your body's current energy levels. Cravings redirect your breakfast plans, bringing you back to the grocery store for a nourishing alternative. Unexpected traffic, making you late for an appointment, grants extra time to absorb an inspiring podcast episode. Creative blockages nudge you away from creating art and towards finding inspiration in the work of others.

In these moments, it's natural to feel defeated and upset. Your well-laid plans seem to crumble, and your ego, accustomed to mastery, stumbles in the face of unpredictability. It loves to control things yet instantaneously loses the capacity to do so. You planned accurately, truthfully and strategically, and now, everything is all over the place. It's not how things were supposed to go. *My growth is hindered and my progress is interrupted and now I'm falling behind.*

Yet, there lies a crucial distinction between planning for structure and planning for control. The desire for discipline, productivity, human connection, thoughtfulness, and intentional living is genuine and warranted. You crave the satisfaction and pride that comes with keeping the promises you made to yourself.

In today's world, however, success seldom emerges from excess. Overthinking, overdoing, overplanning, overvaluing, and overpacking—all are manifestations of overkill. The pursuit of abundance often leads to the dilution of intention and purpose, drowning the essence in a sea of unnecessary extravagance.

Therefore, the question looms—does this desire for control limit or empower you? Is meticulous planning enriching your life with the results you seek or is it blinding you to the untold treasures hidden within unexpected moments? Are you following what you believe you need to do or are you attuned to what your mind, body, and soul are genuinely asking for? It's a delicate balance between structure and spontaneity, between discipline and openness, to the beautiful surprises life unfolds.

Faith's Hymn

Pray, as it's up to God.
Listen, as the Universe echoes back.
Believe, as it's already yours.
Act, as your efforts shape fate.

You Are The Creator

Start every single day with this unwavering belief: *"Today will be a great day."* Even if your rational mind hesitates, continue to declare it anyway. Acknowledge that the following hours may be hectic, or that your circumstances will test your strength, or that you have a to-do list that looms large. Yet, despite the inner voices of doubt, boldly affirm this truth into your core. With each repetition, you're not merely hoping for magic—you're creating it. You begin to observe each experience as a potential gift from the Divine. You open your mind to receiving good fortune, joyful experiences, surprising news, funny encounters, and small moments worth celebrating.

As the night sky descends and you reflect on your day, a sense of satisfaction will wash over you. With a heart full of gratitude, you'll realize that the day's greatness didn't just happen—it was crafted, moment by moment, with your own hands. *"Today was great,"* you'll whisper with a victorious smile, *"because I chose to make it so."*

A Lesson On Life

Seize each moment with open arms, regardless of what it holds. Allow yourself to dynamically adjust to life's rhythm, contracting and expanding as the situation demands. Never regret the love you've given, as it reflects the depth and richness within you. Place your energy on those who elevate you, the people who unleash your inner child-like giddiness and sense of wonder. Find joy within the minutes spent getting from one place to another, or the minuscule instances that shape your evolution towards your brighter future self. Be curious about your heart's weight and your body's aches, seeking understanding and enlightenment. Be equally be curious at the spectacle of life, especially when it unfolds into something far greater than your wildest dreams. Foster soul-filling connections that energize you, leaving a glow of vitality long after you leave their presence. Focus less on your name and material possessions, and more on the richness of your experiences and relationships.

This is the essence of serenity—a state of glory and awe for everything in the present, recognizing each second as a precious gift of life, and fully immersing in the abundance that each moment offers. It's in this presence and openness that your perspective on life is beautifully transformed—one that empowers you to rewrite your story, where you are the architect of your destiny, building bridges to a future filled with endless possibilities.

Monologue for the Soul

Be the type of person who brings out the best qualities in others. Be the force that brings disparate souls together, closing the gap between isolation and connection. Be the radiant energy that makes individuals feel truly seen and wholly accepted. Be attuned not only to spoken words but also to the unspoken emotions reflected in facial expressions. Be the catalyst urging others to chase their dreams, even when the sought-after reality appears distant. Be the one who doesn't take things personally and instead embraces opposing perspectives. Be the cultivator of an environment where others can authentically reveal their true selves, fostering a space for them to express their unfiltered truth. Be the caring hand extended to friends, even when their lives seem perfect on the surface. Be the challenger of peers, encouraging them to perceive alternative viewpoints. Be the constant source of light and energy, regardless of silent struggles.

Above all, be the embodiment of unconditional love—a living testament to the infinite reservoir within each of us. In doing so, you metamorphose into the conductor orchestrating harmony amid the tumult of life.

The Wise Man

If you are able to wake up everyday confident and proud of the decisions you're making, the people you're accessing, the habits you're nurturing, the boundaries you're placing, and the places you're exploring, then trust me when I say this: *you are doing better than you think.*

Your Heart Knows Best

Regret is an inevitable essence of life, it will always be part of the fabric of decision-making. When you choose to move in one path, there will always be a voice in your mind wondering what could have been if you chose differently. Once we understand this as the reality of decision-making, we must also realize that whenever we have to make a choice—whether it be grand or minimal, to stay or let go, to be vulnerable or hold back, to be gentle or rash, to explore or stay put—we must choose the one that feels intuitively aligned *and* holds the regret that we can live with.

Can you shift your career and tolerate letting go of your current identity, or can you stay in your job and live with the fact that you never followed your dream? Can you choose to walk away and make peace with how you never told that person how much you loved them, or can you express your raw feelings yet accept the possibility of rejection? Can you be cruel with your words and bear the repercussions that follow, or can you lead with love and grapple with never receiving a heartfelt apology? Can you push yourself to move cities knowing that discomfort might be felt, or can you stay home and wonder who you might've become if you took the leap?

When you let your intuition and the inevitable regret lead your choices, you will gain clarity on what action will bring you the most peace—in the present moment, and for the rest of your lifetime.

You Are The Placebo

After dedicating fifty minutes to a transformative meditation, I connected and converged deeply with my higher self. She emerged as a beacon of pure light, her presence a fusion of grace and power. Her energy didn't just touch souls; it awakened them. Every word she spoke resonated with profound wisdom, each smile she shared was contagious, and every creation she birthed was a testament to her boundless creativity. This encounter wasn't just inspiring; it was a revelation, compelling me to capture and embody this extraordinary version of myself.

She is strong, confident, and passionate, a woman who knows her worth and trusts that she can manifest anything. She's kind, patient, and trusting, always believing she's exactly where she needs to be and that all of her prayers will be answered in Divine timing. Her focus is on herself—always striving to achieve goals that feel aligned, acting in ways that feed her soul. She doesn't obsess over her health because that was a chapter of the past, and her radiance is a testament to how she takes care of her mind, body, and spirit. She doesn't hold back and instead, says what's in her heart without the fear of rejection or being seen. She achieves great success but in the journey to get there she also celebrates her triumphs, always owning and being proud of them. She acknowledges her progress the same way others do. Her body and soul feel light; the heaviness was a sensation of the past that she's fully let go of. Imposter syndrome is a hurdle that she's overcome, because she now knows her voice is unique and impactful, a voice that no one else can ever mimic. She loves deeply and unconditionally, towards others and herself. She radiates excitement over nervousness, exudes confidence over intimidation, and embraces vulnerability over superficiality. She thanks God throughout the day, for she knows she is always being guided and protected by her unwavering faith. She is no longer surprised by her success because deep within her, she trusted she could do it all. She places bets on herself because she knows she will always win. She never fails to express gratitude. She chooses to believe that everything happens for her and that there are lessons within every experience. She has learned to quiet the negative chatter and instead, feed the positive thoughts. She is at peace. She is full of life. She is radiating. She is love.

While I stood mesmerized by the remarkable person I had described, I had to ask myself a series of simple yet profound questions—why had I ever doubted my inherent qualities? The recognition of my own worth, the kindness that flows naturally from me, the depth of my unconditional love, and my innate sense of gratitude—weren't these traits already a part of who I am? This realization sparked a deep reevaluation of my self-perception, leading me to ponder: Am I not already the embodiment of this ideal version of myself, simply awaiting my own acknowledgment of this truth?

The following morning, I revisited that sacred meditative realm. This time, filled with newfound clarity and awareness, the experience transformed. No longer was I merely conversing with my higher self; I became her, viewing life through her enlightened perspective. The roles had reversed, a testament to my deliberate choice to embody the essence of the woman I had so vividly described. What occurred was a moment of revelation, an epiphany birthed from the depths of my own intuitive wisdom. I imparted a truth to my present-day self that resonated with the core of my being: *"We are one and the same, and you hold the power to access this enlightened state whenever you choose."*

From that moment forward, I have journeyed through each day as the living embodiment of my higher self. What began as a conscious endeavor has seamlessly evolved into the natural essence of my existence.

I believe this feeling is what it's like to love yourself as God has always loved you.

Closure is not an endpoint but a threshold to new beginnings.

In the depths of yet another meditative trance, I found my-self seated on a weathered wooden bench, gazing out over a green expanse of grass beneath a pristine blue sky. The scene unfolded within the confines of a transparent cocoon, a glass box that held me suspended in the present moment.

To my left stood a door made from glass, a portal to the bygone chapters of my life. Through its transparent surface, I witnessed the intricacy of every challenge and beautiful experience I've endured, each moment formulating my current existence. On my right, however, there was a different doorway. Enclosed by an impassive white wall, this mysterious portal concealed its secrets. No glimpse of the future or its possibilities revealed themselves. It stood as a blank canvas, a puzzle yet to unfold, shrouded in the uncertainty of what lay beyond.

In another exchange with my former self, the 26-year-old navigating a life with a chronic illness, she asked, *"What's next for us?"* A reflection of innocence and desperation lingered in her eyes, oblivious to the wisdom I had since acquired. Locking gaze with her, I stood reso-lute, a proud embodiment of the strength forged through overcoming our adversity. With every word that escaped my lips, I embodied ultimate resilience, painting a vivid picture of triumph over the shadows of uncertainty that once shrouded her.

"I'm not sure...but what I do know is that there's a door over there, a gateway to the future, which is evidence that a new and better chapter awaits. And I know this, because to our left is the door that you walked through, therefore you are proof that we endlessly travel through dimensions, always leading ourselves to something greater. It was through you

and your efforts that I am here, as this version of us. And so if you brought me here, then I have faith that I'll bring us there."

Gesturing towards the distant door, I continued by saying, *"And one day, I'll sit with the higher version of me on this bench overlooking a similar view, asking her the same question you just asked me. And even though she'll have more wisdom and more experiences, I have a feeling she'll respond with the same answer. Because the truth is, there is always another door to walk through. Even as we approach the culmination of our life journey, there is a door to Heaven waiting for us to enter."*

It's time to be brave, time and time again.

To shatter the chains of habitual patterns that have been your barriers, embracing a moment of stillness before action, an instant of pause, is key. By asking a deceptively simple yet powerful question to yourself, *"What would my higher self do at this moment?"*, you ignite a process of deep introspection. This question isn't merely a thought; it's a catalyst that sparks a massive shift in perspective.

In those crucial seconds of contemplation, clarity emerges from the depths of your inner wisdom, a luminous guide distinct from the shadow of your ego. This moment of insight unveils the hidden webs of subconscious beliefs and habitual patterns that have silently shaped your existence. It's a revelation, a clear vision of the immense power that lies within you to transcend and evolve beyond these limitations. It is in that moment where you have the ability to make a new choice, bespoke to the patterned decisions that led you to that very moment.

This practice isn't a one-time act; it's a journey of awakening. With each pause, each moment of self-awareness, you embark on a liberating path. It's a process of unshackling, a gradual freedom of the self from the self. This journey is transformative, a renaissance of the spirit, where you're not just living but evolving, not just existing but flourishing. Embrace this path and watch as you experience a metamorphosis where you bloom into the fullest expression of your being.

Just Get Right To It

Recognizing the depths of your misery might be a slow and challenging process, but it leads to a powerful awakening: the realization that you are the architect of your life. Accepting this also means you must confront the truth—that you are your own roadblock. Upon this revelation, ask yourself, *"When will I choose to stop living in this shadow of discontent?"*

Your soul isn't just longing for existence; it yearns for a life filled with meaning, brimming with joy, and overflowing with abundance. This state of bliss isn't a distant dream; it's a potential reality, hindered only by your reluctance to step beyond the familiar confines of your current life.

Deep within, you hold a vivid vision of the life you aspire to—surrounded by people who uplift you, engaged in experiences that enrich you, exploring places that captivate you, immersed in love that fulfills you, and building a career that inspires you. You possess this profound clarity, yet you find yourself treading a path misaligned with your true desires, tethered by the false safety of the known.

The moment of realization is a call to action. The instant you acknowledge that you've been clinging to comfort rather than embracing growth, you're poised at the brink of transformation. This is your turning point. Lean into it with courage, step forward with determination, and embark on the journey to align your life with the aspirations of your truest self.

This is your path to liberation, not just towards a life you desire but one envisioned for you by your higher power.

It's enough for me.

In the depths of my constant struggles with health, I clung to the belief that once my well-being was restored, an all-encompassing radiance would cast away the shadows from every facet of my existence. I intricately linked my vitality to the potential for success in my work, the flourishing of my relationships, and the blooming of friendships. The pursuit of healing led to progress where symptoms waned and my life's quality soared, yet an elusive void still persisted within me.

As my soul energetically aligned with newfound energy, a paradox unfolded. Thriving in various aspects of life, I found myself haunted by an unbearable grief, a mourning for a spiritual loss of my past self. Amidst yearning for the next chapter, where health wouldn't be the protagonist, I grappled with an indescribable ache, infiltrating my days unexpectedly and randomly.

I discovered that severing ties with an identity forged in suffering is one of the hardest aspects of healing. Feeling compassion for my past self that brought me to this moment clashed with the urgency to let her go so that I can just step towards a new future. But how do you release someone when all you ache for is to comfort and whisper to them, *"I am safer now"*? How do you detach yourself from all that you've known? The realization struck hard: attaching my well-being to a specific condition creates a barrier within consciousness. Happiness becomes contingent, a mirage forever out of reach, constantly looping me in a trap of expectation and disappointment. Even upon reaching the coveted destination, a lingering discontent persists. Because the reality is, that part of myself, just like my inner child, will forever be within me. Therefore, what purpose is there to halt living, if that day will never actually come?

Acknowledging this truth, I embraced the notion that fulfillment and peace are not reserved for destinations but must permeate throughout the journey. Genuine peace is not from having everything, but from wanting nothing. True sense of contentment is found in the sufficiency of the present moment.

In the crucible of self-reflection, the pivotal question emerges: *"How can I wholeheartedly embrace and find solace in this very moment?"* The gravity of this inquiry lies in its power to transform perspective, urging us to unearth tranquility not in an uncertain future but within the reality of our current existence.

GENUINE PEACE IS
NOT FROM HAVING
EVERYTHING BUT FROM
WANTING NOTHING.

Sometimes, you uncover a layer of truth,
only to discover that it wasn't the entirety
of the truth God wanted you to see.

The downloads I have received during my morning meditations have never been short of extraordinary. Following a week shrouded in the shadows of a low vibration and resorting to old beliefs, I ascended into the spiritual realm, where I stood in the radiant presence of my higher self. With a warm gaze, she inquired, *"What's bothering you today?"* This query, a key to unlocking my vulnerabilities, prompted me to dissect the precise emotions lingering within.

"I don't quite know," I replied. *"'My health is better, my career exceeds imagination, and love envelops me. Yet, a subtle sadness is lingering in me, perhaps stemming from the heartbreaking pressure and grief that comes with letting my old self go."*

In response, she posed a transformative question, an invitation to delve deeper into self-discovery. *"What if the urge of letting go is not a mandate, but an opportunity to love those facets of yourself? Perhaps the actual burden is the heavy belief that release is a necessity. Isn't that the actual weight on your shoulders? Maybe that's what's consuming you."*

This profound insight sparked a revelation where I asked her, *"Do you still hold those aspects of our past selves?"* seeking assurance. With unwavering conviction, she passionately expressed, *"Of course! I leverage them judiciously, tapping into their power when needed and discarding them in moments where they no longer serve."*

It dawned upon me that my frustration stemmed from a futile struggle to sever ties with elements of myself. What if genuine liberation lay in embracing and accepting my entire being? Rather than shunning those aspects, what if I learned to love and wield them to my advantage in circumstances they'd thrive in? Control, impatience, fear, anger, and stubbornness, though seemingly detrimental, had, in fact, propelled me forward in myriad ways in various experiences. Perhaps the essence of unconditional self-love lies in recognizing and honoring the multifaceted nature of our existence and the role each aspect played throughout our lives.

The realization unfolded—the letting go I sought was not of timelines, healing, or past selves. It was the liberation from the belief that something must always be released in order to fully move forward.

Ironically, in our pursuit of wisdom, we erroneously believe we have absorbed every lesson, only to discover that the true thrill lies in the perpetual cycle of becoming and unbecoming. These powerful moments unveil the intricate magnificence of the human mind, body, and spirit. Life's allure emanates from the revelation that, just when we presume to have exhausted the depths of experience, magic transpires. We are reminded that extraordinary mysteries continuously await, beckoning us to explore the boundless wonders of our existence, time and time again.

By Your Side

Our intuition is an invincible force, a quiet yet unwavering inner voice that guides us with an unexplainable certainty, transcending logic and evidence. It is a subtle nudge in the psyche, allowing us to perceive beyond the visible, to trust in the unseen validity of our deepest senses.

At times, our intuition speaks with crystalline clarity—our actions, infused with intention, shape reality as envisioned. Deciding to stay, knowing a bond is destined, we speak our truth, and paths converge once again. Urging to change direction in our careers, we might soon find ourselves living the dream we dared to imagine. Choosing to relocate, we may discover a new life that resonates with every fiber of our being.

Yet, there are moments when our intuition speaks in soft murmurs—a knowing that something more awaits, though its form remains elusive. We may return to past loves, shift our professional paths, or venture to new cities, only to face outcomes that diverge from our deepest desires.

In these times, we may falter, doubting the accuracy of our inner compass. Was our intuition mistaken? Was it a genuine instinct or merely wishful thinking? But such doubts arise from a fixation on the destination rather than an appreciation for the odyssey.

Consider this: perhaps our intuition was accurate, just not in the manner we anticipated. It sensed an unfinished chapter, a lesson not yet fully realized. It understood that within that relationship, career move, new environment or other pursuits, there lay hidden insights waiting to be discovered. Our intuition doesn't miscalculate; it beckons us toward growth, understanding, and the profound journey of becoming. In light of this, let us gently and relentlessly acknowledge our intuition as a trusted friend, guiding us softly yet surely to where we belong.

OUR INTUITION
DOESN'T
MISCALCULATE;
IT BECKONS US
TOWARD GROWTH,
UNDERSTANDING,
AND THE PROFOUND
JOURNEY OF
BECOMING.

The Artist Above, Volume II

Although I had to walk away from him, it was his unintended lessons that guided me to a fuller understanding and love of myself. Through him, I discovered the boundless level of love I held within me, now ready to be shared with another. During our time together, I shattered the chains of subconscious fears and doubts, realizing that my independence was not a barrier, but a strength. I peeled back layers of my own soul, discovering that I am more than capable of forging deep mental, physical, and emotional connections. I re-evaluated the ways I used my spare time, guiding me to explore new hobbies and experiences that brought me lasting joy. I learned that true connection lies in feeling safe and challenged by someone who awakens and nurtures my inner child, revealing the playful, giddy aspects of my being. I unearthed the power of my own aura, acknowledging the radiance I bring to the table that acts as a magnet. I overcame my own obstacles by learning how to speak my truth, embrace vulnerability, and set boundaries. His essence became a beacon, guiding me to the truth that such connections are not just possible, but are a part of my very being. In his presence, I discovered that the perfect partner encompasses not only the qualities I actively sought but also those I never knew I needed, shedding light on the deeper dimensions of companionship that would be essential to a life-long partnership. Though he may have been unaware, he was the catalyst for a deep awakening in me, imparting invaluable lessons in intimacy, resilience, and self-empowerment. Despite the fact that we parted ways, he brought to light the insurmountable love residing in my heart, and for that, my gratitude towards him is eternal.

Normal People

Looking into the eyes of someone you admire and saying, *"I must let you go now, so that you can find yourself independently of me,"* is the greatest gift we can give to one another, as it honors their journey as much as our own.

Then, expressing appreciation by saying, *"I am grateful for all that you have done for me, for allowing me to look deeper internally and heal what needed to be healed,"* is the greatest level of gratitude we can offer, as it acknowledges the mutual growth and healing fostered through your bond.

Admitting, *"You may have broken my heart but you changed me for the better,"* is the greatest realization we can land on, as it recognizes the silver lining in heartache, the transformative power of love and loss.

Affirming, *"I want you to thrive and become the person you've always dreamed of,"* is the greatest level of support we can express, as it's wanting the best for them, regardless of how it aligns with our own desires.

Finally, declaring, *"I will always admire you, and despite it all, I am still grateful that God brought us together, because He did really good things for us through one another,"* is the greatest form of acceptance for the role you both played in each other's lives, as it celebrates the journey shared and the lessons learned.

Whoever you become and whoever they become, wherever you go and wherever they go, always remember that no person is sent to you without reason. Send them love, give yourself compassion, and feel gratitude towards the magical orchestration of intimacy by the powers above. Through each soul you meet, you are offered a unique chance to evolve into a being overflowing with appreciation, blessedness, and tranquility. These experiences are not mere coincidences and your memories must not be forgotten; for they were the pivotal moments shaping who you were meant to be.

Somatic Purpose

The only difference between the present version of your-self that lacks inner peace and all future versions that flow with ease is quite simple: they allow boundless love to flow in, both from within and from the world around.

To love oneself and to be loved means to accept all that you are and all that you are not. It suggests that you've forgiven all that you've done and all that you did not know. It entails feeling compassion for all the sides you show and all the sides you hide. It implies respect for your choices and the reason for making them. It means allowing your heart to express its truth and feel deeply without any judgment towards all emotions.

Without the ethereal thread of love, what purpose do our victories serve? Can success truly be defined with-out someone, even oneself, to share its glory? Imagine health devoid of cherished connections, a hollow echo of well-being. Contemplate financial freedom without the warmth of human bonds, an empty equation yearning for companionship.

As you delve into the embrace of unconditional self-love, a revelation unfolds—the core of your being is a seamless continuum with your future selves. While they may dwell in realms filled with ease, success, financial abundance, family bonds, and grand adventures, the very spirit, the soul, the essence that defines them is not radi-cally distinct from the luminosity that resides within you at this very moment.

John 3:16

Imagine standing before the Divine, given the chance to ask God *"Why?"* behind all of your life's challenges. Picture Him responding with a gentle clarity and explanation, offering solace with depth and meaning. Would you, in that Divine moment, gracefully accept His reasoning?

Take a meditative pause, allowing the weight of this contemplation to settle in your spirit. Let the question linger, prompting you to explore the depths of your emotions. As you reflect, consider what His truth might be, and whether understanding it could help you embrace the experiences He has given you.

If, even with a clear understanding of His reasons, you find yourself grappling with lingering sentiments of resentment, anger, or frustration, recognize that these emotions serve as gentle nudges to embark on a deeper inner journey. They extend as an invitation to dive into the depths of your soul, to understand why certain aspects of His plan may feel challenging or triggering for you to accept.

Often, our quest for understanding overlooks the essence of God Himself. We seek reasons for the unfolding of events but forget to seek a deeper understanding of the Divine. Amid life's ups and downs, there is one constant—the boundless, steadfast, eternal love that emanates from the Divine source. Welcome this truth wholeheartedly, and you will find that the pursuit of understanding transforms into a surrender to the higher plan. Beyond the need for comprehension, you begin to accept that every facet of your journey, be it joy or suffering, all stems from a place of unconditional love, all to build your character in the way He intended so you can confidently embark on the plan He's laid out for you.

Within this realization, your entire life perspective undergoes a seismic transformation—a powerful shift that marks the moment you unearth the boundless source of eternal peace within, trusting that whatever comes and whatever is taken away is all in the name of complete and utter love.

LET GO OF THE IDEA THAT
THE PRESENT MOMENT
SHOULD UNFOLD IN ANY
OTHER WAY THAN THE
WAY IT CURRENTLY IS.

Let go of the idea that the present moment should unfold in any other way than the way it currently is.

More often than not, our deepest struggles don't arise from the present circumstances but from the dissonance between reality and the narratives we've woven around them. If you were to ask yourself now, *"What is the actual problem I'm facing at this moment?"* listen closely to the whispers of your intuition. It might reveal that the overwhelming challenge lies not in the current situation but in the stark contrast to the tale your ego insists upon. The crushing weight, the disorientation, the paralysis—these may not be inherent to the circumstance but rather products of the narrative you've clung to. It's not the external event but your visceral response that defines your ordeal.

Eight months post-surgery, I remained ensnared in a web of relentless affliction. Undoubtedly, the quality of my life had ascended, yet lingering imbalances returned—evident in my body's protest against food, my skin's inflammation, and the swelling in my pelvic region. Despite my exhaustive efforts, from spiritual rituals to dietary overhauls to diverse healing approaches, I was feeling much better than where I started but I still hadn't experienced ultimate relief. It seemed as though managing my health resembled a game of whack-a-mole—just as I addressed one issue, another would inevitably surface.

I fought the inevitable truth as hard as I could—that I needed help. The conviction that self-medication and self-healing could elevate me beyond this constraint fueled my resistance. A daily contradiction haunted me—should I surrender my control and do nothing, or embark on a quest for new doctors and healers in pursuit of elusive answers?

God's messages will persist until your ears are willing to hear them. I discovered that what I initially thought was me surrendering, was actually me resisting the path God wanted me to walk on. Throughout this time, well-meaning friends and family members suggested new doctors and healing protocols. Yet, having traversed a decade of exhaustive attempts, I often brushed aside their advice. My body bore the scars—both literally and figuratively—of countless procedures, doctor's visits, and tests, leaving me physically and emotionally depleted. The thought of embarking on another quest for a new physician or enduring another six-month supplement regimen or re-telling my lengthy health story filled me with dread. I was overwhelmed with fear and anxiety at the prospect of another procedure. The weariness from past failures haunted me, making it difficult to fathom starting anew. Yet, for an inexplicable reason, it eluded me that my friends and family served as Divine messengers, guiding me with utmost significance on where to tread and what actions to take.

Stubbornly, I clung to the belief that my surgery held the panacea for all my health tribulations. The mere suggestion that I might be wrong, that my grandmother's guidance and the encounter at the airport hinted at an unexplored path, felt unbearable. Did my surgical intervention fall short? Was I misguided in deeming it the ultimate solution? *Was I wrong about...all of it?*

The breaking point arrived when the nature of my existence became undeniable. Each day unfolded in erratic unpredictability—mornings of vitality sharply contrasted with afternoons of incapacitating sickness. A kaleidoscope of self-perception ranged from radiant reflections to a face marred by cystic acne, from carefree meals to the fear of consuming a simple banana. The pendulum swung between feeling light and clear to the suffocating weight of congestion and bodily pressure. A relentless cycle of variability persisted, and yet, I found myself trapped, yet again, in a perpetual state of fight or flight.

Now, the battlefield extended beyond the realm of physical symptoms; it waged a war on my consciousness. Armed with the knowledge accumulated on this arduous journey, I found myself grappling with existential questions. Was this ailment a mere physical affliction, or a manifestation of my thoughts and emotions? Could the remedy lie within the recesses of my mind, or did I require external intervention? In the face of having exhausted every avenue, uncertainty cast a shadow on my path. What plea should escape my lips in prayer, and in the echoing silence, I found myself asking, *"God, are you still there? Can you hear me?"*

As the year drew to a close, I reluctantly acknowledged the need for external aid. The solitary pursuit had its limits. I reached out to myriad new doctors, relentlessly seeking referrals and meticulously plotting out a calendar filled with future appointments. Yet, a nagging sense of defeat lingered. How did I find myself back in this cycle? Why, after all this time, did I stand once more at the doorstep of doctors, tests, and the relentless quest for clarity? The juxtaposition with those around me, effortlessly cured by a single procedure or a simple dietary change, fueled the flames of frustration. I grappled with the inexplicable persistence of this chapter in my life, despite investing every ounce of effort and not witnessing enduring results. Why was this struggle still woven into the fabric of my existence?

The most challenging aspect of this enduring saga was the intricate dance between my intuition and the narrative to which I clung. How enchanting it would have been if my surgery marked the definitive conclusion, the ultimate salve for my wounds. Enveloped in that story, any deviation from its script became a perceived problem in my reality. But I decided that I must be willing to start again, to try anything and everything, and ultimately put my ego aside. God's plan was far greater than mine, and I needed to deeply trust it.

In the wake of this internal conflict, I sought refuge in the offices of new doctors. Gradually, revelations unfolded, affirming that my intuition hadn't led me astray—the surgery did yield results and was the answer to my prayers, but in a manner distinct from my initial expectations. *It didn't miscalculate; it beckoned me toward growth, understanding, and the profound journey of becoming.*

Beyond the physical transformation, the healing journey post-surgery gifted me strength, unwavering faith, and resilience, vital tools to navigate the tempests that continued to assail me. In the shadows of my past, patience waned, my innate strength lay dormant, and the very essence of resilience eluded me. Yet, as months passed, I found myself not only with a stronger body but also with a liberated soul. The surgical journey I undertook transcended mere physical healing; it mended the very fabric of my spirit, breathing life into a wounded soul that had long failed to recognize its power and its worth, not just in health but in all areas of life. The trajectory I embarked upon was not merely a pilgrimage toward self-healing; it evolved into a magical quest that gave me knowledge, wisdom, and insights, now crystallized into the very words written on these pages. Prior to the procedure, the notion of penning my vulnerability at this level seemed inconceivable and my relationship with God was vague, let alone worth talking about—a revelation that now graces the very narrative you are reading.

Then, like a miraculous download, a day arrived when acceptance wrapped its arms around me. I acknowledged that this, with all its imperfections, was still my life, and it was permissible for it to be so. Deep within, I held onto the conviction that something better awaited me. A future where the trials of today would be mere echoes of the past. I painted vivid images of a life steeped in radiant health, of freely indulging in nourishment, and feeling an unwavering sense of safety within my own skin. The realization dawned that while that day hadn't arrived, I knew one day it would, and I was finally at peace with where I was for the time being. And it was enough for me.

In a twist of fate that bordered on the surreal, a newfound sense of excitement and gratitude began to course through my veins for this uncharted expedition. How lucky was I to have the resources to embark on another quest for answers? How deeply blessed was I to have the means to undergo tests, experiment with new protocols, and collaborate with brilliant minds? How fortunate was I to have all of these new spiritual tools under my belt to help me navigate the storms that will come? What an extraordinary stroke of luck that I could further unravel the intricacies of my body, encounter individuals capable of reshaping my destiny, and continue scripting new chapters of this unfolding narrative to be shared with others. How wonderful had God been to me.

Now, look. The allure of this excitement lay not in the mundane tasks—nobody relishes bloodwork or the jarring routine of ingesting a multitude of supplements at dawn. There's no joy in unveiling medical bills or spending Monday mornings in the sterile hush of a doctor's waiting room. There is no allure in immersing oneself in countless hours of research to uncover the elusive roots of an unknown ailment. No one eagerly anticipates passing on the sourdough bread at a Michelin-starred restaurant, or engaging in the nuanced dance of requesting the removal of ingredients from a seemingly simple dish, or contemplating breakfast choices with the sole aim of minimizing the impending discomfort of bloating. No one commends dedicating the majority of their day to be confined in a bathroom, straining to release the remnants of the preceding day's waste. No one looks forward to the disappointment of canceling plans they were once eager for, as their body signals the need for rest through the presence of painful sensations.

However, the source of my excitement was rooted in the rekindling of hope. It wasn't the experiences themselves that elicited joy—it was the beautiful realization that optimism had returned to me. The sheer power of hope lies in its ability to instill trust—a trust that where I currently found myself was precisely where God intended me to be. Beyond the present challenges, it whispered promises of a grander, superior, and more beautiful existence awaiting me on the other side. That's what enlivened me. That's what kept me going.

THE LOVE WITHIN YOU
BEGINS TO TRANSFER
TO OTHER SOULS,
YET YOU'RE MORE
WHOLE THAN YOU
WERE BEFORE.

Yellow Roses

When you begin to love yourself unconditionally, not only does your entire world change, but also the world of others. Each morning becomes filled with vitality, as you revel in the simple joys of mundane tasks and simple routines. With the pulsating beats of your favorite song, you dance through your apartment, catching glimpses of your beautifully messy reflection in the mirror, clothed in ragged pajamas and a wide smile.

Venturing into a grocery store, your soul, filled with vibrant energy, guides you to the flower section. Here, amidst a sea of blooms, you choose yellow roses—not to mark an accomplishment, but to celebrate the extraordinary essence of your existence. As you walk through the produce department, your aura radiates light and love, compelling you to share a moment with a stranger. The grocery clerk, captivated by the bouquet in your cart, acknowledges the significance and expresses, *"It's so nice to buy flowers! Are these for yourself?"* With a nod and a smile, you reply with, *"And for no particular reason, just to give myself some love!"* The exchange continues when the clerk voices, *"I love that! Beautiful color, too. You know, I'm gonna do the same after my shift finishes, I deserve it!"* You walk away, leaving a trail of love behind.

In the structure of your weekends, a Friday night unfolds not as an isolated choice to stay in, but as a deliberate act of self-compassion. Your mind and body harmonize, sending signals that they need rest, not born out of loneliness or a lack of plans, but awareness of your inner rhythms. With compassion as your guide, you embrace this night of rejuvenation, free from regrets or judgment, recognizing the priceless value of restoring your energy and listening to your intuitive voice.

As the next evening dawns, your energy, rekindled and ready to be shared, takes center stage. Admiring yourself in an outfit that seamlessly balances confidence and comfort, you stand before your mirror, the canvas for your self-expression. Bumps across your skin become mere nuances as you affirm that your appearance is the least interesting facet of your being. Stepping out into the world and being seated in the backseat of a stranger's car, rather than drowning in the isolating embrace of headphones, you choose curiosity as your companion. You spark a conversation with the driver, asking them where they're from and what led them to their ride sharing job. They reveal a narrative woven with tales of yearning to fulfill the American dream, distant children, and a marriage stretched across oceans. Sensing the absence of passion and joy in their voice and instead, one filled with loneliness and fear, you become a beacon of celebration, acknowledging their accomplishments, kindness and grit. *"You should be proud of yourself! Life is hard, but you're working towards your dream,"* you kindly express, before saying your farewell as you arrive at your destination. The next rider may be immersed in their own world with headphones on, but they're unknowingly contributing to a subtle shift in the driver's perception of their own life—they now feel more at peace with where they are and embrace the upcoming moments. The love within you, an ever-flowing stream, transcended and touched another soul.

Beneath the open sky and radiant sunshine on a beach, you are no longer entangled in the web of envy or wishful bodily comparisons. You find solace in the imprints on your skin—the streaks on your legs and the scars on your belly. In these silent markers of battles fought and won, you honor these beautiful reminders of your resilience and strength. Each scar becomes a source of empowerment, a celebration of the endurance of your body. This newfound self-awareness extends beyond the surface. No longer content with only admiring the external beauty of strangers, you've mastered the ability to see the internal light that radiates from their aura. This shift in perspective becomes a mirror reflecting the light you now see within yourself. In every encounter, you express acts of kindness—a smile, an open door, a genuine compliment—actions that transcend mere gestures, becoming conduits for deeper human connection.

In the midst of a bustling gathering surrounded by unfamiliar faces, you engage in a dialogue with a stranger who is clearly living a life vastly different from your own. Though their story may be foreign or uninteresting, you remain invested in their narrative. Unrelenting in your curiosity, you ask questions, your eyes locking with theirs, capturing the enthusiasm that spills as they discuss a passion that animates them. You, too, have been on the other side of this exchange, where excitement coursed through you as you shared your dreams or recounted a personal victory. The sensation of someone embracing every word, every expression, is etched in your memory. In extending this grace to another, each question becomes a lifeline, every minute an affirmation for them. The person before you feels not just heard but deeply seen and validated, echoing the yearning you've known in your own moments of passionate self-expression. In this exchange, the love within you becomes a bridge, linking hearts and souls, linking who you once were and who you are now.

In the depths of late-night conversations with close friends, where life updates unfold—proposals, dream jobs, and budding romances—you not only extend congratulations but immerse yourself in their triumphs, absorbing the sheer exhilaration as if it were your own. The absence of these achievements in your own life no longer echoes as a void; instead, it transforms into a wellspring of joy. These moments cease to be markers of what's lacking but rather become a celebration of the thriving lives of those you care about. Your capacity to share in their pleasure transcends the superficial, weaving a connection that validates and acknowledges their growth and victories, and is a testament to the steadfast presence in one another's lives. In the exchange of joy, a ripple effect takes hold. As you offer genuine recognition, the person in front of you feels not only acknowledged but celebrated, solidifying the foundation of their journey and where they've arrived. This act, seemingly simple yet incredibly genuine, allows them to delve deeper into their own salutation, where their newfound self-love and acknowledgment create a ripple, a cascade of positivity that extends beyond the immediate circle, igniting a trail of love that echoes in the relationships they share with others. They now begin to celebrate others the way you've celebrated them.

In the pursuit of your own dreams, the yearning for external validation dissipates, and the need for proof that you tread the correct path becomes irrelevant. Liberated from the constraints of self-doubt, you unabashedly share your triumphs and the abundance they bring through a balance of confidence and humility. Amidst the narrative of personal achievements, where belief in your potential manifests into reality, you emerge as a guiding light for those around you. Your journey becomes a testament, encouraging others to heed the call of their own souls and embark on paths that resonate with their deepest aspirations. In the future, a time unfolds where distant acquaintances, inspired by your example, venture into the uncharted territories of their dreams. In these moments, you release the desire to showcase your latest achievements, redirecting the spotlight solely onto them. Expressing genuine pride and excitement for their destiny, you ask about ways to offer unwavering support. As the conversation shifts, you become more than a distant observer; you transform into a steadfast cheerleader. Their gratitude echoes, acknowledging that your support was the catalyst for their bold choices and how without your encouragement, they might never have taken the steps toward their desires, never reaching a place of alignment, vitality, and joy.

And so what these experiences demonstrate is that when you begin to love yourself unconditionally, not only does your entire world change, but also the world of others.

The love within you begins to transfer to other souls, yet you're more whole than you were before.

BE YOUR OWN SAVIOR,
FOR IT IS THROUGH
DISCOVERING GLORY
AMID THE TRIALS
THAT RESILIENCE
FLOURISHES.

Do you want to be the victim or the victor?

We all experience our own unique form of suffering. Some carry the weight of chronic pain etched into their bodies by illness, while others bear the indelible marks of childhood traumas from fractured homes. Substance addictions and emotional dependencies wrestle within some, while others grapple with financial hardships or the silent battles against isolation despite outward success. Faces bear the scars of bullying, whether inflicted by others or self-inflicted due to societal expectations. The grief of losing a loved one is felt by many, yet some mourn those who are still walking on this earth.

We all have been there, are there, or will be there— experiencing some form of hardship. This is the reality of human existence. Rather than wishing away or succumbing to anger, it is crucial to recognize that harboring resentment only robs you of your power, happiness, and inner peace. Acknowledge that suffering is an intrinsic part of life, and in this realization, you have the opportunity to find humility and uncover glory within it. Navigating the labyrinth of distress is not about mere survival but about embracing the power within to thrive because of it. Be your own savior, for it is through discovering glory amid the trials that resilience flourishes. Hope, when transformed into action, becomes a force of creation.

Look around and contemplate the influential figures in the world or the impactful individuals in your life. Behind their strength and success lies a narrative of suffering; it is from the crucible of pain that the strongest souls have emerged. They are the characters who are seared with scars yet continue to traverse this world with boundless joy, gratitude, and serenity. They radiate compassion, welcome the present moment, and exude a vibrant aura because they have unlocked the profound truth about suffering: *pain will push you until your calling pulls you.*

You were placed on this earth for a reason, therefore you must reflect on your own narrative—do you wish to remain the victim of your circumstances or do you aspire to emerge as the victorious architect of your destiny? The choice is yours.

My soul chose my body for a reason.

Throughout this introspective journey, I found myself entangled in the belief that my mind, body, and soul were distinct entities, each leading its own existence. This perceived separation birthed a constant disconnection within, an unsettling void that lingered.

Yet, amid this internal turbulence, I discovered deep admiration for my soul—the radiant core that guided me through each day, infused with an ethereal glow of light and love. Once burdened, my mind evolved into a superpower through deep introspection, paving the way for monumental breakthroughs. My thoughts transformed into spoken words, resonating and leaving an indelible impact on every soul I encountered. However, I still held a sense of bitterness towards my body, like an awkward companion in a social circle. It seemed an outsider, not fully embraced, yet providing moments of joy that compelled us to acknowledge it nonetheless.

The concept of this perceived separation began to captivate me. Where does the mind truly dwell—in the brain, the heart, or the gut? And where does my soul find its abode—within every inch of my body or nestled within my chest?

Contemplating my spiritual experiences, those that left me in awe, tapped into my inner knowing, and connected me with the Divine, a subtle yet obvious realization dawned on me. Every spiritual encounter and transcendental experience, born from the imprints of my soul and the awareness of my mind, manifested through my body. It has always been the vessel for miraculous sensations, emotions, realizations, experiences and intuitions. Why, then, did I persist in viewing my mind, body, and soul as distinct entities? They were in constant communication, sending signals—guiding, urging, and compelling me to experience, feel, and embrace. How, then, could I continue to ever resent my vessel that allows me to have such a vibrant, rich and remarkable human experience?

With this integration of understanding, my healing underwent a metamorphosis. I began to connect the fragments of myself that had long been disconnected, embracing a sense of wholeness that brought peace, enveloped me in acceptance, and allowed a deep sense of safety from within.

Gone are the days of resentment toward my body. Even when waves of painful sensations crash, when the echoes of swelling revisit, or the purges of vulnerability spread across my face, I welcome them with open arms. I've deciphered the silent language my body speaks, a language yearning to be seen, heard, and validated through the symphony of pain and the ballet of love. In the past, my response was laced with harsh words and deep-seated hatred, a discord that echoed through time. Now, a symphony of gratitude accompanies every ache and twinge, thanking my body for revealing the truths and wisdom I'm meant to receive.

Within this understanding, gratitude replaces resistance. The mere sensation of pain becomes a rendezvous with my mind and soul, working in unison to unveil the messages rooted within. No longer do we bear the weight of burdens; we soar into the realm of freedom. My love for myself has shed its conditional shackles, blossoming into a non-conditional intimacy. The once separate entities have seamlessly merged into a harmonious oneness, a beautiful synthesis of mind, body, and soul.

Just when you believe you've reached the depths of God's surprises, a revelation unfolds, taking the awe to even greater heights.

In November 2023, I felt compelled to share the story of those two strangers I met in the bustling heart of Atlanta's airport online. With raw emotion, I spilled the enchanting tale of Divine magic that had unfolded, leaving me in awe of God's exquisite handiwork. Despite pouring my heart into a video that I shared on social media, the response was lukewarm; the engagement modest, the viewership scarce. Undeterred, I clung to the belief that the right eyes would find it and that it might wield some meaningful impact. And then, life unfolded.

Two months later, a message arrived from an un-familiar soul. A 23-year-old beauty, also grappling with the agony of Endometriosis, stumbled upon my video. In the depths of her own suffering, both physical and emo-tional, she felt nudged to reach out to me in desperation. Mirroring my own journey, the mystical significance of '444' resonated deeply within her.

This young woman, six months post-op, struggling against resurfacing physical pain and dwindling mental health, asked me for guidance. Her prayers, once filled with light, had evolved into desperate pleas shrouded in anger and resentment. *"Why, God, why?"* echoed through her pain-laden cries.

As I consoled her, she explained that she was on the brink of despair, shackled by a body that prevented her from experiencing more in life. Her faith in a higher power shattered and she stood at the crossroads of hopelessness. It was in this dire moment that our connection, seem-ingly orchestrated by Divine forces, unveiled its purpose. In a twist of fate, we discovered that the surgeon who had operated on her was the very same one recommended to me by the woman I had met at the Atlanta airport. No mere coincidence, but a cosmic alignment that bound us all together for a greater purpose.

My role in this newfound connection became clear—to be a beacon of light and a vessel of hope for a soul drowning in darkness. I shared every ounce of wisdom, sharing the spiritual tools and daily practices that had guided me to a place of peace, acceptance, and better health. Despite her loss of faith, my words and genuine compassion became a Divine sign, a glimmer of hope that she too could emerge from the depths of despair. But not only did I offer her optimism, I provided love—for herself, for the journey and for the higher purpose it all serves.

The following morning, I reflected on the cosmic threads that wove our destinies together. It struck me with crystal clarity—she was a reflection of my former self. Her thoughts, beliefs, and patterns mirrored the past I had once struggled to escape. God, it seemed, had orchestrated this meeting to showcase my evolution, revealing how drastically my thoughts had transformed, how I had reshaped my subconscious beliefs, and finally found acceptance. He gave me physical proof that the work I had been investing in myself was indeed working.

I also noticed that God had granted my long-held desire—to reconnect with that past self. My meditations and the spiritual realms allowed me to experience those supernatural moments, but it only extended within my mind and never in my reality. This beautiful soul, a mirror of previous versions of me, allowed me to verbally share the transformation I once never thought was possible. In these fleeting exchanges, I became a guide not only for her but for the 'past' version of myself dwelling within another soul, here in the physical world. The advice I was offering was everything I wish I could've shared with the 26-year-old version of me.

This unexpected encounter wasn't just about changing her life; it was about transforming mine. God had sent me this soul to illuminate a deeper purpose in my health journey—to guide others toward realizing the boundless power of love within and all around. My role on this earth had never been clearer, as I embraced the profound impact of a seemingly chance connection that turned out to be a cosmic masterpiece.

Be the spark that ignites the flame within others.

Perhaps I have won the cosmic lottery. I was given the honorable task to be here on this earth, at this time, in this body, with this mind and with these gifts. I was given the astonishing journey of immense suffering that led to sublime greatness and wholeness. I am living proof that the words etched thousands of years ago—*you do not realize now what I am doing but later you will understand*—are still true to this day. I am proof that transformation is not only possible for all, but available to each of us if we dare to embrace it.

I may hold the winning ticket, but the Universe offers infinite lotteries, each presenting its own chance for greatness—reminding us all that within every soul lies the potential for a transformational miracle.

What you're looking for is not anywhere else other than inside of you. Can you truly trust yourself?

After riding a wave of high frequency energy and placing my trust in God's higher plan, I found myself yet again in a place of defeat. Another blow struck in the form of a health setback, filling my soul with sensations of agony, confusion, and unrest, despite all of the efforts poured into body, mind, and spirit alike.

At first, I resisted despair. I clung to the belief that there was a higher purpose to the pain I was experiencing and that there would be a profound lesson hidden within the turmoil. I chose to keep going, reminding myself that God had a plan beyond my comprehension, hoping that with each passing trial, my soul would find healing, and thus, my body too.

I listened intently to the whispers of my body, engaging in a constant dialogue to decipher its cryptic messages. This newfound harmony, this unity of mind, body, and soul, was a massive win for me—a blossoming bond suffused with compassion and love. Yet, as days stretched into weeks, my hope waned, and confusion started to bubble up. The grip of illness tightened its hold, with no sign of my symptoms getting better. But I refused to surrender the beauty of life to the shadows of affliction, so I mustered the courage to place myself amidst the company of friends and in environments that brought me bliss. The lesson—*to not travel too far from joy*—had been learned long ago.

Ironically, five weeks prior to this very moment, I had booked a future session with a Medium, yearning to reconnect with the essence of my departed grandmother. As all things do, God's timing for this session unfolded right in the midst of my tribulation, where my grandmother's presence could offer a beacon of comfort and solace for my clouded mind. She spoke of guidance, protection, and a nurturing embrace throughout my journey. The details that she provided were unfathomable, where only her and I could know the significance and the meaning behind them. She praised the resilience I had cultivated and the unwavering faith that had weathered storms, urging me to hold fast, to trust, even in the darkest hours.

Though the session was special and touching, as the call ended, a bitter taste of disappointment lingered. My questions regarding my health journey were met with vague responses and my quest for clarity shrouded in uncertainty. All I had heard were simple truths—that I was on the right path, doing the right things, and at the right time.

My ego sank into a pit of defeat—despite the passage of time, the accumulation of experiences, and the countless beliefs I've reshaped, why did this feeling persist? Frustration gripped my heart, casting a shadow over the future, as I grappled with surrendering to a higher purpose, doubting the wisdom I thought I'd internalized. It felt as though all I had learned, all the words I'd etched into the very pages of this book, were suddenly rendered meaningless.

In desperation, I kneeled and turned to prayer, tears filled with fervent pleas, seeking understanding, seeking strength. *"God, please show me what I am missing. Let me understand what the purpose of that session was, and the broader significance of everything I'm currently experiencing. Please, let me hear your voice."*

I had come to love this aspect of myself—where despite any and all pain, rather than walking away from my faith, I was compelled to deepen it. This place, position and release of emotions that was once a burden, had now become a moment of deep solace for me. The more I prayed, the more I cried, the more I released, the more I surrendered and the more I felt free. And in that moment, what initially felt like an exorcism became another pivotal moment of deeper awakening. *How many can a 27-year-old girl have within nine months?*

Gazing into the mirror, I confronted my reflection with newfound resolve. The purpose of my communion with my grandmother was not to unveil the mysteries of the future or unearth the secrets of the past; it was to kindle the flames of self-trust, to illuminate the path of intuition unfolding before me. The answers I was seeking did not lie in the ethereal whispers of the beyond, but within the depths of my own being. But by searching for answers beyond myself, I had neglected the wisdom within my own mind.

Everything that I had heard during that session were thoughts and beliefs that I had already written in these pages. In simple terms, I already knew that I was on the right path, that I was doing everything right, that this point in time was providing more expansion of my soul, that I must find more self-compassion and grace, that there is a deeper purpose to it, and that where I was was aligned with God's Divine timing and plan. I already knew that the harmony of mind, body, and soul was paramount to true wellness, and that my journey held the power to ignite inspiration and healing for others. I already knew that I hadn't gone through all of this for nothing, that God will deliver on my deepest desires when the time is right.

Suddenly, I found myself locked in a gaze with my reflection, and like a mantra, the words spilled forth: *"You keep searching because you don't yet fully trust yourself. So now, you need to trust yourself. You need to trust yourself. You need to trust yourself."* In that moment of clarity, I realized that if all the answers resided within me, there was no need for further seeking or questioning. If all that my grandmother conveyed were the truths already known in my soul, then wouldn't that mean that I already possessed the strength, truth, and resilience to navigate the challenges of life? The energy once spent in pursuit could now be redirected towards embracing the innate wisdom and intuition that lay dormant within.

The next day, I found myself reflecting on countless instances where my intuition had proven true. From sensing shifts in energy around others to seizing career opportunities, from being in the right place at the perfect time to speaking up when needed, from making dietary choices based on my body's cues to selecting the right healthcare professionals. Each time I followed my inner voice, my reality seemed to fall into place, and clarity washed over my mind. So I had to ask myself, what could possibly make me believe that my intuition was not to be trusted? I unknowingly quieted the voice of the parent within me, the voice that exuded tranquility, strength, unwavering compassion, and boundless resources, and instead, fed the voice of my inner critic and ego.

There is a question that still nags at me—how many times must we revisit the same lessons before they truly sink in? Now, as I navigate this setback in my health and reflect on my encounter with my late grandmother's spirit, I understand their deeper significance and why this lesson hadn't been learned fully by this point in time. It's a continuous non-linear journey of healing not just for my body but for my mindset too.

If I can fully trust myself in this realm, in matters so deeply personal and vital, then surely, I can rely on my intuition in every facet of my life. I'm reminded that the dreams I wish to manifest, the connections I seek to foster, the career I yearn to develop, and the paths I yearn to explore all require the steady guidance of my inner voice.

Therefore, I had to re-encounter this lesson at this point in time, and truly let it sink in, before I experienced the next chapters of my ever-evolving life. Perhaps learning this lesson at that point in time, signified that something far greater awaited on the other side. *Amidst the chaos and despair, deep down we know that every setback is followed by a remarkable comeback.*

It is in moments such as these that I am humbled by the ineffable ways of the Divine. For in every trial, in every moment of doubt, He offers solace, clarity, and unwavering guidance, a testament to His boundless love and infinite wisdom, only if we dare to ask and listen. He orchestrated the timing of that session, weaving threads of fate weeks before my need became apparent, ensuring its culmination at the precise moment of revelation. This is exact proof of Divine Timing.

YOUR RESILIENCE ISN'T
MEASURED SOLELY
AT THE SUMMIT; IT'S
CREATED DURING THE
JOURNEY ITSELF.

Intelligence

F. Scott Fitzgerald famously wrote: *"The test of a first-rate intelligence is the ability to hold two opposing ideas in mind at the same time and still retain the ability to function. One should, for example, be able to see that things are hopeless yet be determined to make them otherwise."*

When life becomes turbulent, tossing you into intense waves of despair, it's natural to feel overwhelmed. Doubt creeps in, shrouding your vision of hope, leaving you questioning your own strength despite all of the mountains you've conquered before. But remember, your resilience isn't measured solely at the summit; it's created during the journey itself, every step a testament to your unwavering spirit.

During the chaos, conflicting voices beg for your attention. On one side, everything feels unjust and you challenge the fairness of it all. Yet, within the noise, there's also a gentle whisper, a voice of reason and resilience. It speaks of purpose through the chaos, promising a breakthrough beyond the struggle.

How do you navigate these paradoxes? How do you rise above despair and embrace the uplifting voice within? Perhaps the answer lies in accepting the duality of your reality, in acknowledging that both darkness and light can coexist, that both can be true.

Yes, life may seem unfair, but you can also trust the events are happening for you. You can do everything right without reaping desired results, and believe there is a day that you will have everything you seek. It's a journey of contradictions, where the darkest nights pave the way for the brightest mornings.

Can you find strength in this delicate balance? Can you embrace both despair and hope, without judgment or rejection? And can you be determined enough to defy hopelessness, refusing to let it define your destiny?

This ability to reconcile opposing viewpoints demonstrates a high level of cognitive agility and emotional resilience. It requires a deep understanding of nuance and a willingness to embrace complexity rather than succumb to binary thinking. Ultimately, intelligence is not just about understanding, but also about action and perseverance in the face of challenges.

It already has happened.

When you wholeheartedly embrace the whispers of your inner voice, you're enveloped in the conviction that each cherished wish and every fervent dream has already happened in the timeline of your life. In this unwavering trust, doubt and anxiety dissolve into insignificance. For if the Universe has already orchestrated the fulfillment of your desires at some point on your timeline, what is there to fret over?

Our truth is left for all untold.

Have you ever noticed that the majority of our thoughts are either focused on the past or future? We hardly ever think about the present moment. If we do, it's either because it distresses us or because it is so beautiful that we feel mournful that it's a fleeting moment in time that will soon become the past.

Though each of our thoughts throughout the day can vary widely based on individual circumstances, personality traits, and current situations, there are common themes in people's daily thoughts that we universally give our energy to.

We often think about our short-term and long-term plans, including tasks we need to accomplish, goals we want to achieve, and future aspirations. Thoughts about daily responsibilities such as work tasks, household chores, and errands are quite common. We often mentally organize our to-do lists and prioritize those that need our primary attention. Thoughts about family, friends, romantic partners, and colleagues are frequent. We may ponder our interactions, worry about conflicts, or simply reminisce about enjoyable moments. It's common for us to have worries and anxieties about various aspects of our lives, including finances, health, relationships, and career. These thoughts may range from mild concerns to more significant sources of stress. We often engage in introspection, reflecting on our emotions, behaviors, and decisions. We might assess our strengths and weaknesses, evaluate our progress toward personal or professional goals, or contemplate ways to improve ourselves.

Thoughts about hobbies, interests, and leisure activities provide moments of enjoyment and relaxation throughout the day. We might anticipate enjoyable experiences or reminisce about past enjoyable moments. The human mind can wander into various creative and imaginative realms. We may have random thoughts, creative ideas, or flashes of inspiration unrelated to our immediate tasks or concerns. Expressions of gratitude and appreciation for life's blessings, such as good health, supportive relationships, or moments of joy, often occur spontaneously throughout the day. Amidst the hustle and bustle of daily life, we frequently think about opportunities for rest, relaxation, and self-care. We might look forward to moments of downtime or plan activities to recharge. Thoughts about upcoming events, whether they're social gatherings, vacations, or milestone occasions, often occupy our minds as we anticipate and prepare for these experiences.

If we observe our daily thoughts as they come and notice that they're robbing us from being in the present moment or are taking away our precious energy, then we must ask ourselves, *"Do I need to think about this right now?"* If the answer is no, detach from the thought the moment you realize you haven't. If the answer is yes, continue giving your energy to it. In essence, everything you "think" is going to happen, or has happened, is just a story you're telling yourself. If it hasn't happened yet, then there is no point in speculating. If it already has occurred, bring yourself back to the now to unravel the meaning of it. If it's going to help you in a positive way in some future time, then go on.

In doing this practice, I assure you, you will realize how many thoughts flow through your mind that you actually don't need to think about. That is when you allow yourself to truly live, not just survive. Because rather than planning how to be happy or reminiscing times you once were, you just become happy, here in this moment.

**We all arrive at the same understanding but
the way in which we learn life's lessons vary.**

Suffering is a universal aspect of the human experience, manifesting in various forms, both physical and emotional. Whether it's physical pain, emotional pain, grief, existential angst, psychological pain, trauma, social isolation, domestic violence, injustice, oppression, addiction, substance abuse, societal torment, relationship conflict, childhood trauma, and so forth. Yet, each trial, each tribulation, serves as a teacher, guiding us toward a deeper understanding of ourselves and the world around us, and illuminating the path toward healing, growth, and ultimately, redemption.

We can all agree that change is the only constant in life. Everything, from joyous moments to painful experiences, is transient. This impermanence can lead to a deeper appreciation of the present moment and a greater sense of acceptance.

We can all attest that life is filled with challenges and setbacks. True strength is not in avoiding these obstacles but in how we bounce back from them. Resilience is the ability to adapt, persevere, and grow stronger in the face of adversity.

We know that finding meaning and purpose is essential for a fulfilling life. It's not always about grand achievements but also about the small, meaningful connections and contributions we make to the world around us.

We believe that human connection and relationships are fundamental to our well-being. Building and nurturing meaningful connections with others enriches our lives and provides communal support during difficult times.

We trust that understanding oneself—our strengths, weaknesses, values, and motivations—is crucial for personal growth and fulfillment. Self-awareness allows us to make informed choices, cultivate authenticity, and live in alignment with our true selves.

We can conclude that compassion is the ability to empathize with others, to understand their struggles, and to offer kindness and support without judgment. Practicing compassion not only benefits others but also brings a sense of fulfillment and interconnectedness.

We discover cultivating gratitude involves recognizing and appreciating the blessings and abundance in our lives, no matter how small. Gratitude fosters a positive outlook, resilience, and a deeper sense of contentment.

We trust that accepting life as it is, with all its imperfections and uncertainties, is essential for inner peace. It involves letting go of the need for control and learning to embrace reality with openness and equanimity.

We are aware that living authentically and pursuing our dreams often requires courage—to step outside our comfort zones, to face our fears, and to persevere in the face of unpredictability. Courage allows us to live with integrity and purpose.

We are conscious that the present moment is all we ever have. The past and future are illusions, giving us a sense of identity and a promise of what can be. But the more we focus on time—past or future—the more we miss our lives that are in the now.

The wisdom I've learned along my path was delivered through the vessel of physical affliction, yet I can assure you, the essence of what you've encountered within these pages echoes the familiar cadence of your own life's journey, perhaps in differing shades or depths. Through shared human experience, we find solace in the realization that the lessons learned by others hold resonance within the chambers of our own hearts, offering a wellspring of understanding amidst our own trials.

It's a liberating revelation, isn't it? To recognize that our individual journeys, while unique in their manifestations, are anchored in the universal truths that bind us all—truths that transcend the boundaries of time, circumstance, and personal narrative.

Perhaps, then, we truly are just walking each other home to where we belong.

Last Look

The moment I knew I had been reborn was when my morning meditations ceased to consist of past or future selves. Instead, I found myself immersed solely in the presence of my current self, realizing that within this moment lay all the solace and guidance I needed.

Gone were the days of reaching out to distant echoes of myself or seeking wisdom from elusive higher beings. Instead, within my meditative trance, I began to visualize myself seated before a mirror, engaging in a heartfelt dialogue with the beautiful person staring back at me. In that sacred space, I posed my questions, and almost instantly, the answers came flooding in. It was a communion of sorts—a celebration of victories, a sharing of fears and joys, a nurturing of dreams. But the transformation didn't end there. Now, as I open my eyes and pass by any mirror, I pause, smile, and engage in conversation as needed, and always end with, *"I love you so much."*

This profound shift didn't occur by chance; it was a conscious choice, a deliberate act of embodying self-love and self-trust. I came to understand the value of trusting my own intuition and ceased the futile search for answers outside of myself. This included letting go of the habit of consulting past or future versions of myself that no longer existed or were yet to come into being. The significance of this evolution lies in its symbolism: my subconscious underwent a profound alchemy, affirming that my present self holds the truth and possesses the wisdom to discern what is right, always.

The seed of angelic freedom, planted months ago, has been tenderly nurtured by patience, faith, and resilience. It underwent a metamorphosis, emerging now as a radiant flower in full bloom. Within the delicate petals of this blossoming symbol, I discover the unwavering assurance that I am enough, I am safe, and that I possess all I need to thrive, here and now.

This is what changing your life actually feels like.

You become aware of the pattern that you must break in order to enter the next level of your being.

You make a decision by shifting your actions from what you've always known to something new.

You begin. One day, one step at a time, you embark on your set plan.

You feel discomfort and question your ability to continue. Part of you wants to resort back to the known, yet another trusts that freedom lies on the other side. Despite the opposing voices, you listen to the parent within you.

You fall backwards, only to realize that you no longer belong there. *This is the confirmation that your soul is ready for evolution.*

You tread forward. Day by day, decision by decision, action by action. Your reality may not reflect massive shifts, but your energy and mindset have evolved towards lightness, peace and gratitude. That's the only proof you need to keep going.

You flow. You may begin to notice shifts in your physical reality, through people, experiences or aligned opportunities.

You embody a new way of being. What once was a deliberate decision, has evolved into an intuitive existence.

You become aware of another pattern that you must break in order to enter the next level of your being.

The cycle beautifully continues.

Beginner's Mindset

No matter how advanced you get, continue to stay open to new experiences and new ways of living. The wisdom you've acquired thus far might not be everything there is to know. The experiences you've had to date might only have scratched the surface of what your soul's path is meant for. The thoughts you currently think, the beliefs you currently hold, and the patterns you currently partake in might one day need to be altered, shifted, or broken. Embrace this with excitement, for this is what makes life interesting. With a beginner's mind, there is no limit to what you can explore, what you can learn, or who you can become.

I didn't think this day would happen.

I hope one day you can stand before a mirror, gaze into your own eyes, and declare with unwavering conviction, *"The journey was tough, but look at us now—we made it."*

Father Ocean

I am profoundly grateful
That I didn't end up with what I believed I wanted
Or what I thought I needed
Because what I received
Has been far greater than any of my desires
In embracing this newfound abundance
I yield to the Divine plan
For I know it will surpass
The limits of what I can

I Can See Clearly Now

"How much more can I take?" I pleaded, my voice trembling.

"My child, can't you see?" He responded with an unwavering tone.

"See what?" I questioned, searching for answers.

"Each trial I give you is to reveal how strong you are," He expressed with purpose.

"But what am I doing wrong? Why is there always another hurdle to conquer? How much more can I take?" I argued with frustration in my voice.

"Because you haven't realized it yet," He replied.

"Realized what?" I asked.

"The unlimited power within you to overcome it," God declared, His voice carrying the weight of truth that had been waiting for me to fully embrace.

EPILOGUE

If I were to encapsulate the essence of this journey in a single sentence, it would be this: within the waiting period between asking and receiving prayers lies the alchemy of transformation. It is in the shield of patience and resilience that our true selves are refined, our aspirations take flight, and our faith is restored. Those are the moments you not only realize your potential but also start to become it.

For too many years to count, my most fervent prayer that echoed countless times a day was: *"God, please heal me."* Initially, I had a specific vision—radiant health, lightness, energy, no physical pain, normalized digestion, balanced hormones, and a healthy relationship with my body. Yet, in response, God whispered, *"I will heal you but in ways you never knew you needed."* Now, as I reflect on the last twelve months, my vision for healing has drastically changed and my perception of what answered prayers look like has evolved.

Reflecting on the 26-year-old version of myself before the life-altering surgery, I gaze back with compassion and love, yet also a tinge of sadness and grief. She possessed wisdom beyond her years, strength unnoticed, love unacknowledged, capability unbelieved, success uncelebrated, and light unrealized. Now, at 27, in a complex metamorphosis, those limiting beliefs and subconscious thoughts have dissipated—I have learned to honor the mind that was given to me, to recognize the strength that I hold, to embrace the love that I was built upon, to believe in the capacity my body has, to jubilantly celebrate the success I've achieved, and to exuberantly praise the radiant light that now emanates from within me.

Although I can confidently now state that I am living freely and with vitality, God's healing touch transcended mere physical restoration—it reached the spirit within, my soul, my essence. The beauty lies in the fact that, at a mere 27, I have bravely confronted and triumphed over a multitude of demons; the kind that might consume others over decades in arduous battles, often leading them to inflict pain onto others or to give up on their life. However, I have skillfully harnessed their essence for the greater good of all; turning my pain into purpose and my journey of transformation as a beacon for others.

Yet, life stretches expansively before me, promising continuous healing, patterns to shatter, and wisdom yet to unfold. The journey ahead remains an unwritten canvas, inviting the question: who will I become in the next year, five years, and beyond? What storms will be sent to me, not to destroy me but to cleanse me even further? What blessings are on their way and what will manifest that I have yet to even think about? The allure of the unknown is enchanting, for I believe that the person I evolve into through its mysteries is precisely who God intends for me to become.

ACKNOWLEDGEMENTS

To God: For a considerable stretch, I unknowingly held resentment for the path you set before me. However, standing in the reality of my present existence, I now feel an overwhelming sense of gratitude for the life and the gifts you have blessed me with, and that you've chosen me to share the magic they've brought. Though the journey has been demanding and taxing, it was through my faith and the unwavering trust you planted within me that I have emerged triumphant. My health, the beacon that demanded my attention on you, serves as a constant reminder that your presence will envelop me throughout this lifetime, and as the catalyst to foster deeper healing for others.

To Yaya: The sky looks different knowing you are up there. In the acknowledgements in my first book, I expressed gratitude with the words, *'Thank you for all that you have given me, and continue to give me, despite not physically being here.'* Little did I know the extraordinary journey that would unfold from that moment. Your invisible shield of protection and guidance not only kindled hope but also facilitated significant healing I once deemed impossible. When you were alive and felt helpless, you desired to assist in any possible way. I hope you know that you've surpassed that promise. In ways beyond my wildest imagination, you have given me more than I could have ever dared to fathom. You have shown me colors I never knew existed. *You have given me a new life.*

To Romen, Talar & Alek: You, the radiant orbs at the center of my Universe, my steadfast anchors, the source of the deepest unconditional love I've felt. Through this painful journey, you've been my mentors in holding onto the battlefield within, navigating fear, embracing love, facing loss, defying darkness, sustaining faith, and finding joy amid it all. You, the three souls ever-present, continuously lifted me, preventing any descent, always seeing me through the highs and lows of it all. For this, I'll be forever thankful that God chose you to be my family.

To all of my past selves: I find myself frequently reflecting on the myriad versions of us that have traversed time—those I've distanced myself from and those I've wholeheartedly re-embraced. In those quiet moments of contemplation, I delve into the depths of our vulnerabilities and the glorious summits we've scaled. I dwell on the breaking points, where despair threatened to consume us, and the turning points that rekindled the dormant flames of our resilience. Yet, I now realize that altering even a single thread would unravel the intricate design of my current life. Because despite the arduous path we've been on, look at where we stand today—we've emerged triumphant. We've reached a destination we once deemed unreachable, and it's all a testament to your unwavering efforts, your boundless dedication, and your steadfast commitment. Thank you for leading us to this harmonious present moment.

To my future selves: May the flame of the unlimited power within you burn ever brighter, guiding you through the twists and turns of your evolving journey. Never lose sight of the intricate beauty woven into every step and let your vulnerability be a source of strength that transforms not only yourself but also the world around you. May your awe and wonder, for both the vast external Universe and the intricate depths of your soul, only grow stronger with time. The prospect of witnessing the incredible person you are becoming, the feats you achieve, and the ripple of impact you leave in your life fills me with boundless excitement. *I look forward to meeting all of you.*

To the incredible souls who walked alongside me: From cherished old friends to newfound companions, from the compassionate spiritual guides to the dedicated doctors, you are forever woven into the tapestry of this healing journey. Each one of you holds a unique place in my heart, the threads that intricately bound my path toward wholeness.

To name a few: Dr. Joe Dispenza, Dr. Ulas Bozdogan, Mary Spirito, Matt Gottesman, Katie Sabbaghian, Annalie Howling, AJ Alvarez, Tracey Shepard, Gina DaCruz, Jeanne Grey, Bella Cataldi, Emma Boyd, and countless others.

To all women who suffer from Endometriosis: My heart resonates with the depth of your struggle, yet within that ache, I find excitement for the extraordinary woman you are destined to become on the other side. Describing this relentless affliction feels like grasping at elusive words, unable to capture the full weight it thrusts upon us—both the physical toll on our bodies and the silent trauma etched into our minds. This is more than a physical ailment; it's an unwelcome intruder seeping into every corner of our existence—our thoughts, our work, our relationships, our dreams. Whenever you feel alone, know that I stand beside you. In moments of stagnation, trust that a higher force is gently guiding your path. Surgery, while a crucial step, only takes you so far. The true remedy to this affliction is a treasure already within your grasp, free and ever-present: *love.* It's an arduous task, loving a body that seems to betray you, but let that be your starting point. Physical restoration will unfold, but the true healing lies in the love you cultivate within yourself. It is the beacon guiding you through the shadows towards angelic freedom.

To you: My only wish is that you truly realize the unlimited power within yourself. May my story be a beacon, guiding you to not only feel inspired by my transformation but also to embark on your own journey of self-discovery and unleash the extraordinary potential that resides within you. Embrace the strength, resilience, and boundless capabilities that make you uniquely powerful. Open your heart to God, to the Divine powers that orbit you, and the love that surrounds you. Let my narrative serve as a testament to the incredible heights you can reach when you believe in the limitless possibilities within your own mind, body and spirit.

To all of my friends, family, and community, your endless support and encouragement will never go unnoticed. I feel incredibly blessed to wake up each morning with the kindness that surrounds and envelops me, and that God brought you all into my life in the way that He has. Thank you for showing me that love is the powerful force that is the root of all forms of healing.

Thank you.
Thank you.
Thank you.
I love you all.

Today, yesterday, always, and forever.

Xx
Karin

Karin Hadadan is the author of 'Beauty in the Stillness' and the creator behind ICI ET NU (translated from both French and Danish, which means 'Here and Now'), which both champion the transformative power of living in the present moment. Her path to self-realization and healing has been a testament to the alchemical process of turning pain into purpose. Through the intersection of mindfulness and spirituality, her words and art inspire others on their own paths of self-discovery by offering a reservoir of knowledge, wisdom, and actionable insights. She's a first-generation Armenian and Assyrian soul residing in New Jersey.

instagram.com/icietnu